Beyond Beautiful

BY SALLY MILLER
WITH DARIN DURAND

L'Edge Press
PO Box 1652
Boone, NC 28607
ledgepressnc@gmail.com

ISBN: 978-1-935256-82-3

Cover Art: "Trinity in Resurrection." 2020. Sylvia McGuire.
Used by permission.

For all who have experienced insidious trauma against your will, this honest account of how God truly lifted Sally out of the pit will give you hope. From deep seeded fear and lies to flourishing in the Fathers truth, you will find this life story beyond beautiful.

—Becky Joern, Developmental Spiritual Director

Throughout life people come in and out of our lives, some bring pain and difficulties in our path. Others are there to help refine us and challenge us to do better. And then there are those who are sent to walk along side of us and help carry our burdens and our pain with love and grace. All the while showing God's love and goodness and healing power even in the darkness and storms.

Sally is one of those precious women who understands deep pain and sorrow through her own life, but also the great victory and healing that is available to anyone who is willing to go through the darkness to get to light, the powerful healing light of Jesus Christ!

—Eileen Marx, All Things Possible

Being a soul surgeon is a rare gift to be given and stewarded. Having integrity and a deep devotion to God to help people heal and the sacrifices it takes to do this well is just rare. Sally embodies all of this with humility, love, kindness and compassion. Learning of her journey to get there is a very special gift to all of us.

—Victor Marx, All Things Possible

Dedication

To My Dear "Katie"

Dr. Katie Merwin

Friend, companion, counselor

Life raft in times of trouble

Jesus with skin on

Fellow sufferer

Humble servant

Thank You

Thank You

To all my wonderful encouragers — too many friends
& family to mention. If you even think you were one,
you were.

But one edited, encouraged, challenged and cowrote
along the way.

Darin Durand
You are an amazing, gifted writer and such a generous
person. I never would have made it without you, my friend
and brother in Christ. So grateful for you.

Sylvia McGuire
You are a gift to your world in many ways. Thank you for
being so generous with your art on the cover.

Jeff Hendley with Abbie Frease
My dear friends and publishing team. You have offered
indescribable generosity.

And

There was this little writing group that taught me more
than I ever wanted to know about writing. You were a joy
and a blessing to be mentored by.

Table of Contents

Dear Reader

I should either be dead or in a mental hospital. It is only by the grace of God that neither are true of me today.

Growing up, I experienced life in a series of disconnected fragments, like puzzle pieces scattered on the floor. As hard as I tried, I could never make the pieces fit together in a way that formed a coherent picture. However, as I look back over the last thirty-five years, I can now see the beautiful piece of art on the cover of the puzzle box. With a grateful heart, I can honestly say the zigzag journey has been worth every step. Furthermore, I can testify that it was the Savior who not only walked with me but carried me to the place of freedom and wholeness that is now my growing, daily experience.

In those same years, I also endured pain and suffering. This fueled my hunger to pursue truth in the midst of so many lies, dizzying confusion, and betrayal. The tears that once fell from deep sadness and despair now glisten in the light of hope and joy.

Pain and suffering are the Refiner's fire, burning away the chaff. What is left behind is different for every person, but for me what remains is a deep compassion and a resolve to be present to others during their hour of darkness. I have learned that suffering brings understanding and understanding brings compassion.

I hope my story can in some way help you move forward in yours. I hope you walk away from this book having found a deeper communion with the only One who can transform your ashes into beauty: Jesus Christ.

Hold tight to His promises. He is faithful. Remember that He is "close to the brokenhearted; he rescues those whose spirits are crushed" (Psalm 34:18 New Living Translation).

My joy would be complete in knowing that my words have brought you HOPE and spurred you toward HEALING.

The Characteristics of Trauma

I am here to testify about the God who came alongside me when I had no idea who or where He was. He is the loving Father who helped me see that the longings of my heart were placed there by Him; they are legitimate needs, and they are designed to be met.

For years I was unaware of my emotional collapse, primarily because I had lived so long in a hypervigilant state, paranoid that everyone was watching me every second of the day. Landmines littered every situation, and the consuming concern at the forefront of my thinking was, am I safe enough to speak? If I perceived that the people and circumstances of the moment provided safety, then I would speak, but only after evaluating and carefully choosing every word. Not only was it exhausting, but this paranoia caused ulcers at fourteen and a habit of sweating out my inner world through profuse perspiration. Experiencing safety and the peace that flows from it were the exception rather than the norm.

Reviewing my past through the eyes of an adult, I see now that this wasn't normal, so why was I living this way? As I pieced the clues together, the reason eventually came to light. It was the result of deep and severe childhood trauma, which had fragmented my personality.

The way we perceive and process life influences who we become in a powerful way. Everything that happens to us growing up (positive or negative), especially during our first five to seven years, affects our soul, which is comprised of our mind, will, and emotions. Our "heart" is the container that holds these three and is often referred to as the seat of the soul. This is why Wisdom instructs us above all else to "guard our hearts," for out of it flows the quality of our life (Proverbs 4:23).

The conclusions we draw from our experiences fashion a significant portion of our belief system. These conclusions in turn impact our behavior. In this way, our behavior is a reflection of what we believe. Unfortunately, what we believe is a combination of both truth and lie.

During those first seven years of life, we absorb and form conclusions automatically. It isn't until we are older that we start to question and begin the process of "cleaning up" our belief system.

Everyone experiences trauma to one degree or another, and each person responds to it in different ways. Although this may sound contrary to the character of God, it is apparent that when a child goes through severe and prolonged trauma, our Father protects a person's soul by allowing it to fragment. This is a work of grace. The fragmented parts that are created serve differing roles to assist with survival—primarily protection, but also to facilitate day-to-day functioning in the world.

This fragmentation is unknown to the individual until God's grace brings it to their awareness through personal revelation or through someone with the discernment to recognize the signs.

It is naturally confusing to others who can't see that this fragmentation has occurred. For example, my response or survival strategy expressed itself through a lens that said, "If I am perfect enough, I won't get hurt." I adopted this lie subconsciously and it ruled everything I did until it became impossible to maintain. I didn't know this was my strategy, nor did those with whom I was interacting. It was unspoken, yet fully operational.

As a person matures, God's grace brings awareness of the fragmentation and He gently invites the parts to reintegrate, restoring wholeness into a single identity. It's a rebuilding process with Jesus Himself as the chief cornerstone. We all have to go through some degree of this rebuilding process.

However, when severe trauma is involved, it adds additional layers of false beliefs that need to be replaced with truth. These lies tend to fall into four categories: what we believe about (1) ourselves, (2) others, (3) how the world operates, and (4) our Creator.

The degree to which we can function in mature, constructive ways is proportionally related to the number of our beliefs that align with God's truth. Conversely, the degree of dysfunction and immaturity we express is proportionally related to the beliefs we hold that align with falsehoods.

A heart that is filled and overflowing with lies is how I would define brokenness. When trauma remains unresolved and our strategy for coping with the trauma is based on a lie, each day is simply about surviving. The void (absence of truth) inside created by the trauma sucks up all the energy, leaving nothing for the people and activities we love. In our brokenness, we are often left wondering "Why can't I get life to work for me?"

Fortunately, God in His wisdom has provided a powerfully simple and miraculous process for replacing the lies with truth. Biblically, this process is rooted in Romans 12:2 where we are exhorted to take our thoughts captive and align them with God's truth. The Holy Spirit does this all the time for us beneath our consciousness. There are times, though, when we need help to identify the lies consciously, and the Holy Spirit ministers to us through another person's presence and facilitation.

I refer to this facilitation process as inner-healing prayer. It's not complicated. The facilitator asks the Holy Spirit to reveal which lie is in operation and the Holy Spirit brings it to our awareness. Once identified, it is rejected and replaced with God's truth. Many have referred to this as the Great Exchange. It mirrors Christ's willingness to sacrifice Himself on the cross in our place. He exchanged His life for ours. God uses this process to bring healing to the innermost places of our heart and redeems our brokenness.

It was through this process that I experienced reintegration, freedom, and renewed hope. During the long years and countless sessions, God supplied all of my needs and met me each and every time. Lie after lie, layer after layer of deception was removed. Although I couldn't see it, He was maturing me into a functioning adult in His likeness.

He took me back to the beginning and reparented me and then taught me how to reparent myself. I didn't even know that this was possible. My counselor, who has her Doctorate in Marriage and Family Therapy, has been at my side for the last 18 years facilitating this process between the Lord and me. Recently, she told me that I walk in more wholeness than anyone she knows.

As a result of God's grace and healing in my life, I've been able to teach and lead many individuals through this process over the last twenty years, and it always brings some level of healing. It never fails, because it is God doing the work, and I simply get to marvel at His handiwork!

All of this gifting springs from the unexpected fruit which blossomed during my youth—my time in the wilderness. God gave me the ability to recognize and understand why people often hurt other people, even when they don't want to.

Brokenness often expresses itself through behaviors and reactions that result in the exact opposite of what we long for and desire to see manifest in our lives. It was the behavior flowing from my own broken heart that helped me to understand and, therefore, extend compassion towards others who are reacting from brokenness.

I continue in personal counseling and inner-healing prayer, but now my focus is on ministering hope and healing to others. Because suffering gave me such a deep compassion for others, I want to be used as a vessel to come alongside those who struggle emotionally.

The Bible says we are able to comfort others with the comfort which we have received, making us the best comforters. Pema Chodron captures this idea well: "Compassion is not a relationship between the healer and the wounded. It's a relationship between equals. Only when we know our own darkness can we be present with the darkness of others. Compassion becomes real when we recognize our shared humanity."

If my story provides one ounce of hope for what you may be walking through, then the hours and hours of inner healing work will have been worth it. The knowledge that someone else has trodden the path you are on and understands how the fragile mind becomes resilient can illuminate two important truths.

First, you are not alone. Most everyone encounters a season in their life that leads them to contend with the dark night of the soul.

Second, if there are others who have overcome trauma, so can you! You must choose to the walk the path toward wholeness and believe it is possible for you.

Begin now and declare, "I am ready to be whole and live the abundant life promised to me in Christ!"

Pandora's Box

Driving 1100 miles is a small price to pay when you love the ocean as much as my husband does. Our road trips to the west coast provided a rare escape from the day-to-day grind. Growing up in the Rockies, the contrasting view of the ocean, which split earth and sky at the horizon line, mesmerized every part of my being.

The unsettling truth, though, was my sense that if I stepped into the water, I would keep walking and allow myself to simply float out to the horizon until I was unable to return. Fatigue had found a new address and moved in, overcoming me, which seemed incomprehensible at thirty-five years old. All I wanted to do was sleep. There was no rational reason that I could discern.

The friends we were visiting sensed my struggle and were notably concerned. My husband and children were even more so. The kids were just elementary age, but they were worried about their mom. Shortly after I arose each morning, fatigue would drive me back to bed, to watch helplessly as everyone left for each day's scheduled fun. This vacation was not turning out to be what we expected.

Mark was our firstborn. He was strong, athletic, a great student and very responsible for an eleven-year-old. He already knew he wanted to be a teacher and coach, though maybe more coach than teacher.

Mandy was eight and full of life—a joy with a little mischievous streak that led to plenty of funny family stories. A couple we were visiting said, "Boy, it gets critical quick with her, doesn't it?" A little drama queen we decided.

My husband had grown up near the Finger Lakes, becoming an aquaphile, craving water of any kind. Thus, California beckoned. San Diego was idyllic in the 80's, and I wanted to see its beauty and enjoy every part of it. I definitely did not want to be left out of the fun and disappoint everyone, but my debilitating exhaustion left me with no choice. I spent every day of our California vacation in bed.

After we returned to Colorado Springs, my husband and I went to the family doctor. He told me, "You are sick because you are depressed." I replied, "I'm depressed because I am sick." My husband agreed with me, and we immediately changed doctors. But the diagnosis of depression stuck and a new reality set in, involving a "drug trip" no one should ever have to take. Experimenting with anti-depressants is just wrong. There should be a way to bypass the zombie zone in order to find a bottom from which to function.

Clouds of confusion moved in as I faced the very real problem of not being able to get outside my own head. The referral to a psychiatrist from the second doctor felt humiliating. A Major Depression diagnosis forced me past denial. I wasn't crazy, I had been telling myself. I was simply not functioning very well. For depression to physically overtake a person seemed illogical. How could my emotions rule my body?

I had to learn this lesson: we are physical, emotional, and spiritual human beings in one container. Of course emotions affect us physically.

I began to read every self-help book I could afford. Still, most days I couldn't get out of bed. When I could, there was always getting the kids to school, participating in their activities, maintaining a household, trying to function. Numbness joined the clouds, confusion, and debilitating fatigue. Maybe from the drugs, maybe not.

The drugs weren't doing enough. The psychiatrist said people get the most help with both drugs and counseling, so I sought out my pastor for counseling. I knew I needed help but had no idea what, how, or where to turn. A pastoral counselor seemed safe. Still, I could hardly speak in our sessions. I had always been quiet and reserved. The fear of the bottomless pit of pain meant I had to control my emotions at all costs, to hold back my thoughts, which also meant holding back my words.

After crying my way through recounting my fatigue and depression in my first session with him, he simply prayed. As he prayed, I began to see in my mind the ceiling of my bedroom in the adobe hut I grew up in on the farm. The rusty water stains bled into faded orange paint, which was peeling from leaking so many times.

But it wasn't only my bedroom. There were four of us—one older stepbrother and two younger brothers—all sharing the same bedroom. As the pastor continued to pray, a sense of my older stepbrother's weight on top of me came to my mind. I also had the physical sensation of pain and pleasure inside me. At the most, I had been six or seven years old.

I tried desperately to hold myself together in front of my pastor, but I finally broke as reality set in and I let it all spill out. What does a person do with that? My pastor comforted me and suggested that I go home and ask the Lord to bring me some healing. Physically and emotionally shaken open like a can of soda spewing everywhere, I somehow managed to drive home and go to bed.

As I lay there, before I could pray anything, I had a vision of a window into heaven with flowing, sheer white curtains. Looking through, I saw this indescribably beautiful field of flowers, and in the middle was a white-draped four poster feather bed. I was there in a wedding gown, and Jesus was with me. He laid me on the bed like a child, lifted my gown, and wiped me clean with a pure white towel. It was the most vivid vision I've ever seen, and an immediate sense of relief replaced the trauma. A priceless gift. That experience would become an anchor for the healing to come as I uncovered more and more.

I wish I could say that day was the end of it, that it was "one and done." That I was miraculously healed that day, and completely recovered. Instead, that first memory opened a

Pandora's box that I would never have believed if I had not lived through it myself.

Visits to counselors and psychiatrists became a weekly and sometimes twice-a-week occurrence while trying to maintain some semblance of a routine. Life had to go on. And actually, reflecting on that fact now, it helped me in some ways—but I had become lead weight moving in slow motion.

Friends helped too—friends that could genuinely listen, acknowledge the pain, and put some of the confusion into words for me. It meant I wasn't as alone as I felt.

I continued to see my pastor for about two years before my recovery plateaued. My best friend's counselor seemed like a good fit for her, so I followed suit. She had her License for Marriage and Family Therapy and was a good Christian counselor. That began (emphasis on began) the deep work I felt was necessary to recover.

Before my father died more and more memories were coming to the surface. I remembered my grandfather leashing me to a tree like a dog, and locking me in the food cellar next to their house. I had the impression that for some reason, this was all he could think of to "take care" of this little three-year-old toddler. He didn't know what else to do with me. Before my father died in his 70's, he admitted that he treated all of us children like dogs. I guess my dad came by his meanness naturally.

My medications were helping, and I was able to function while still taking time for counseling. My husband, though, was struggling. His biological mother had committed suicide on his first day of first grade, so he spent some time in an orphanage before being adopted by the mentally ill mother who raised him. My depression diagnosis was a huge trigger for all his issues.

He'd had a negative experience with his own counseling over the years, and he refused to pay for mine. I tried to work full time to cover the expense. Many times, emotionally exhausted from crying through whole counseling sessions, I had to compose myself and go back to work. Part of me was able to maintain a façade of being competent and professional. A performance extraordinaire, but every footstep was forced.

Pain and grief kept coming. The counselor would tell me there was a light at the end of the tunnel, and I would reply, "I'll have to take your word for it because I can't see it." How I even kept going for counseling is miraculous all by itself, but I was like a dog on a bone about getting some relief and finding a way out of the hell hole. On some level, I knew it meant life or death for me.

We thought it would be helpful if I spent a weekend at Glen Eyrie, a beautiful castle retreat center in town, to rest and try to gain ground in my recovery. I called my parents the first night to keep them posted but ended up crying through the whole conversation, unable to verbalize much at all. They were so worried. My dad shared his typical infamous advice: I should pull myself up by my bootstraps. But how is a person with a broken leg expected to walk?

I lay there wide awake all night. Insomnia had become common for me, so I always took something to sleep, then something else to get going in the mornings. This time, though, nothing helped. At about 5:30 am, I called my husband to come get me. He came but insisted I drive the car home anyway.

Nothing seemed to significantly help, and functioning was becoming more and more difficult. Checking into the hospital became an option for the first time. I knew it meant the psychiatric ward, but I was so worn down, I didn't care. Thinking my counselor would have to be involved, I called her.

She said, "Sally, you can go if you want to. They will drug you for two or three days and send you back home. You'll be in the same or worse condition as you are now."

Not an option, after all. Looking back, I am very thankful for that decision. Living with the reality of being hospitalized all these years would have made it worse.

Three or four years into this journey, we wondered if it would ever end. Hope for getting well was beginning to fade.

The Farm

In the 1950's and 60's, farming was about survival. My parents had to borrow money every year to farm, and if the farm did not produce, we would lose it to creditors. That kind of stress pushed my father into epilepsy, with grand-mal seizures becoming a regular part of our lives. As I watched, horrified, I never knew whether he would come out of each seizure alive. He almost bit my mother's finger off once when she tried to grab his tongue to prevent him from choking. The doctor suggested she not do that again.

Looking from behind a six-year-old's eyes, growing up in southern rural Colorado, life was harsh, difficult, and cold. The nearest small town made national headlines for the lowest temperatures in the nation. Minus forty-two degrees set a record. Regardless, the dairy cows had to be fed and milked twice a day, every day. Washing the milking machines, cleaning the tank, and sweeping manure out of the barn were the children's daily chores. It's hard to remember a time when I didn't do them.

Occasionally, my dad scraped out the corrals with a tractor, leaving me breathless for fresh air for days. I would cringe when the school bus picked us up, knowing I smelled the same. As soon as the door opened, the smell of manure preceded the mocking comments which were like kernels of popcorn popping up from every seat while I walked in, red-faced.

And then there were the sheep. It took the whole family and the dogs to move them from field to field for different grazing along the dusty roads. The annual shearing filled ten-foot gunny sacks with wool. My father would drop my brothers or me down into the sacks to jump up and down, packing the wool tight.

Chickens were fed and eggs gathered daily. For a single fried chicken dinner, necks were chopped, carcasses dipped in hot water, feathers plucked, pieces cut apart.

And the pigs had to be slopped. This meant pouring the contents of the compost bucket into a trough where the pigs enjoyed displaying their terrible table manners. I still can't eat pork.

Spring brought birthing season for our cattle. Due to the cold and predators, we often found ourselves hand-feeding the orphans with a soda bottle and nipple. My dad once let a calf into the house to be fed. Such investment in their survival always led to me getting attached, only to bear the grief of their loss when they were sold at auction for butchering or other purposes. This has closed my heart toward animals to this very day.

Like clockwork every autumn, my dad and my grandfather drove to the Four Corners—where Colorado, New Mexico, Arizona, and Utah meet—to pick up a truckload of Navajos for potato harvest. They picked by hand, row after row of acres. It took a couple of weeks. During those weeks, they lived in a mud hut with a dirt floor and fire pit in the middle of our property. It's sad to think about now, especially because that was their normal living conditions. Concha belts and turquoise jewelry draped their velvet skirts and shirts, leaving me in awe and wanting to touch. Fear and ignorance prevented me from getting close.

By the time I was eight or nine, I'd learned to drive the trucks. There was a makeshift bumper seat to raise me high enough to see out the windshield, and blocks were tied to the floor pedals so my feet could reach them. I had to help with loading bales of hay and bags of potatoes.

There was always some piece of machinery or vehicle breaking down and needing repair. We kept a tab open at the local John Deere. I recall one day when no one was available to make the run to town for the hay baler part. I was not yet sixteen but I was an experienced driver, so my dad sent me. One of the neighbors saw me. Thinking he was being the "good cop," he promptly drove to our house and ratted me out to my dad. Poor guy went away disappointed.

Somewhere in the midst of every other task, three farmers' meals were prepared each day with a lot of homegrown produce. A strappin' breakfast with pancakes, eggs, and bacon, sausage and ham. A pot of coffee was on twenty-four seven ends up being the local coffee shop. Lunch was another robust affair. My dad insisted that the main, noon meal—dinner—must include meat, potatoes, white bread, and white gravy, followed by dessert. When I complained about being fat, my mom would say, "You're just pleasingly plump." Maybe it was the bread and gravy, sometimes with spaghetti.

I was the second-oldest and the only female of six children, so a lot of the housework, cooking, and childcare fell to me, in addition to the outside chores. My stepbrother was three years older than me, my next brother was two years younger, then a brother seven years younger. When my mom was forty and I was fifteen, she gave birth to yet another boy. Two years later, my dad insisted she have another child so the fifth one wouldn't grow up spoiled rotten. I didn't know any different at the time, of course, but now I realize he was quite the dictator.

My mother was my dad's second wife. His first marriage lasted six months. Since his first wife's name was the same as my mom's—Phyllis—he called my mom "Bernstein." It was the name of the store where we'd bought the sofa. Pretty demeaning if you think about it. Dad also had awful nicknames for my stepbrother, like "Peon." I got lucky: my nickname was "Punkin."

My father was a rage-aholic. Children were to be seen and not heard in the 1950's. One wrong look, and we were toast. No second chances. If he couldn't figure out who did something wrong, we all got punished. A car ride to town was especially volatile. It was common to see us beside the road, all getting a beating because the guilty party, if there even was one, had not confessed.

He was heartless and cruel, purposefully instilling a deep fear in his children to deter bad behavior. A leather two-inch strap or a belt was always handy for the beatings, or he would simply knock us across the room. If we wet our pants, we got beaten for that, too. He picked up my little forty pounds by the collar once and shook me so hard, my shirt tore completely off and I fell.

When you are not safe in your own home, you grow up believing you are not safe anywhere. Being punished whether you are innocent or guilty does weird things to your mind. I didn't have any place to put that, so I think I created a place, unable to make sense of it.

Dad did have a fun side when he wasn't angry. Some nights he would take us through the hayfields in the pickup to go jackrabbit hunting. He let us drive, sitting on his lap, and we would run the spotlight so he could shoot. Pheasant and duck were special delicacies. By age eight or nine, I could shoot most anything.

Dad also found time to play baseball with us since we had enough for a whole team. And there were a few trips to the mountains for fishing and picnics.

A prankster too, he could be quite creative. The closet between the two bedrooms had openings on opposite ends. One night he put a hose in there and made ghost-like sounds. In retrospect, that wasn't exactly fun for us kids.

Where was my mother in it all? After years of counseling, the Lord showed me that she had feared him as much as we did. My mom had trouble keeping up with all that was expected of her. She helped with the farming as well as everything else. Dad would get angry that the house wasn't clean enough and then the raging bull would do it himself. He threw a highchair out the back door once because it was out of place and in the way. In that moment, I knew he would throw me out too, if I was ever in his way.

I never talked back or stood up for myself. The price was too high to pay. Instead, I chose the lowest profile possible, determined to never rock the boat. This became the foundation of a people-pleasing perfectionist for whom survival meant peace at any and all costs.

Believing I never had a say in anything left me in a prison of silence and impotence. Layers of unspoken shame took deep root. Painted across my heart, soul, and mind was the refrain—I have no voice, I am not nor ever will be good enough, and I have no value or worth for simply existing.

Decades later, after I married and had children, Christmas meant returning to the farm. Our kids loved it and were old enough to really enjoy farm life.

On the first trip to the farm after I had started counseling, I began crying during the three-hour drive and could not stop. Once again, the prospect of a fun time for all was looking grim because of me.

When we arrived, I kept telling everyone I had to go back home, even knowing the kids would be so disappointed. Everyone kept asking me what was wrong, but I couldn't answer since I genuinely didn't know. It was unreasonable, of course, but I kept insisting, unable to logically consider the situation. I was like a child demanding her way. They all talked me into spending the night and leaving the next morning, Christmas Eve. By morning, I felt better, so we stayed.

It was years later before I got in touch with the inner child who had genuinely believed she was going back into an abusive situation on that trip. I had acted out of that child-like place—the inner child who was holding all the abuse. Even as an adult, the child still feared going home.

1952
2 years old

1958
8 years old

1968
17 years old

The Family Tree

Family dynamics on the farm were often volatile, with my paternal grandparents living on the same property, a half-mile from our adobe hut. They lived in a 1940's settlement house for which they were very grateful to President Franklin D. Roosevelt.

Memories of my grandfather, Pappy, are vivid still. He would stand at the kitchen door, covered in dust, wearing his bibs and a dirty, sweaty ol' farmer's cowboy hat, smoking a pipe while chewing tobacco. Deafness contributed to the volume of his cursing about anything and everything. I'm sure there were words in between the curses but I never caught them. Everybody referred to him as a mean S.O.B. The depth of his meanness only proved what life had done to him. To find the good heart in him, you would have to peel back layers and layers of tough skin. I always felt that his heart was in there somewhere, but I never got the opportunity to see it.

My grandmother was one-quarter Cherokee. She ran away from Cherokee country in Oklahoma at 14 to marry Pappy. As capable as any man, she survived a heart attack in her 50's. Working the fields, plus preparing all meals from scratch over a cast iron wood-burning stove, handwashing laundry, and caring for two sons while trying to survive the Depression will do that to a person.

I can still smell her scent of rosewater, along with Pappy's tobacco. And I can see her with a bandana wrapped around her head, wire-straight strands of gray hair peeking out. I have fond memories of climbing up on the stool and watching her and her sister, Snooks, making pies and biscuits. The children—or "chillum" as she used to say—knew the treasured bubble gum bowl amply supplied by her would be a sure score.

As the first child of my dad, I was her first grandchild, so her favor seemed to rest on me. I asked her once why she only had two children when most people had several for built-in forced labor (whoops, I mean "contributors to the family business"). She said she'd been afraid to have a daughter. She didn't want a girl because life was so hard on them.

Grammy embodied my only safe place. She taught me the Bible. "Church" meant Oral Roberts on the black-and-white TV. She empathized with how hard I had to work so over-paid me to just wash windows and clean for her. She never left the farm except for the doctor. Her passing wrecked my world.

Grammy had two sons, Bill and Bob. Bob, my dad, was the younger one, and Grammy favored him. He was mammoth in my eyes and in reality—over six feet tall and averaging 200 pounds in the summer and 250 of mostly muscle weight in the winter. His size was enough reason alone to fear him, and he milked it for power and control. I measured how big around his fingers were once, thinking they would be the size of a nickel, but it turned out they were the size of a quarter. He used to torture me by rubbing his red bushy beard in my face.

For only an eighth-grade education, he could figure out anything, eventually building a 640-acre thriving farm. He was a smoker from the time he smoked his first twig at ten.

My dad chose to stay on the farm while Bill started a construction business. Visiting my cousins in town became a treat even though I feared Uncle Bill. He, of course, came from mean as well.

The cousins had the best of the best while I gladly received hand-me-downs from anyone and everyone. The pink shag carpet and white provincial furniture in my cousin's bedroom birthed envy in my little heart.

Shocking us all, Uncle Bill divorced my Aunt Mary for a younger woman after 25 years of marriage. Brokenness is passed along.

***

My counseling sessions seemed endless by now. More and more memories were being uncovered. I realized along the way that God was being as gentle and kind as He possibly could by only giving me one at a time. I wanted so much to be done with it all. But no, He knew that if I remembered everything all at once, I would have a psychotic break from which I would not recover.

Memories would pop up outside of counseling sessions. While driving around town one day, I suddenly got an image of male genitalia in my head. That's all. At my next counseling appointment, I almost didn't bring it up. A little embarrassed, I finally said, "This seems weird, but out of nowhere I saw this picture in my mind…?"

As I began to get more in touch with the image, we both realized it was a memory of my uncle forcing oral sex when I was about five years old. We were at my grandparents' house for a family gathering so it was quick, rushed, over and done. A single threat from him that my mother would die if I told her meant I was committed to keeping the secret forever. Another trauma buried alive.

As with every newly-surfaced memory, I was in disbelief. How could this memory possibly be true? The counselor affirmed its truth because of my visceral, emotional reaction. Looking over all my memories taken together, I too can confirm that it fits the pattern and cycle of abuse that has emerged over time.

And so, back to recovering. But would I ever get there?

Some Light

At least I could go about my life by then, functioning fairly normally. It was progress. I had been in weekly therapy for ten years. How much worse could it get? I felt better, but I did not feel well, and I was determined to be truly well.

Finally, I plateaued with the first counselor. Also, her rate went up to $90/hour which was prohibitive at the time.

My search for someone else led me to a counseling pastor at a large church I had visited. He gave me the names of three counselors. "Pray and ask the Lord which one to call," he said.

The pastor agreed to see me until I had heard from the Lord on the other three names. He also suggested I attend a support group for severely abused people. By the end of the first meeting, I thought, "How could they possible help me? They're more messed up than I am!" I never went back.

I continued with the counseling pastor for a few more sessions. One day, he gently and ever-so-kindly told me, "Sally, I think you might be dissociative."

He smiled at my blank expression.

Leaning forward, he said, "Dissociation is like a fracturing of the brain because of abuse or trauma. A person has the ability to leave their body and watch what's happening, resulting in the creation of different personalities or alter-personalities. It happens because of physical, emotional, or spiritual abuse or trauma, including seeing others being traumatized.

"Technically, it's called Dissociative Identity Disorder, or DID, formerly known as Multiple Personality Disorder."

As I pictured the movie Three Faces of Eve, my heart plunged to my stomach. I felt the color drain from my face. Even though I think he was trying to reassure me, I never heard another word he said. I left with a nauseous headache. I searched for a place to file his diagnosis in my mind.

The conversation with God on my drive home left with me with many more questions. What am I supposed to do with this? It was incomprehensible, but if it was true, I was worse off than I ever imagined. So this is what the bottom of hopelessness looks like. Now what?

Lord, where are you? Do you care? Are you even aware? Could I just get a life raft here? I didn't say any of this in an angry or bitter way, but in the saddest, most lifeless way.

***

"Very high functioning," my new counselor said.

Her name was Laura. I liked her right away and felt safe with her. Out of the list of three counselors the pastor had given me, she'd responded first.

After meeting a few times, I broached the subject of dissociation with her. She didn't think that was a possibility. It took several more sessions and my mentioning it before she agreed to check it out.

At the same time, Laura was just beginning to understand Inner Healing Prayer and finding it even more beneficial than Cognitive Behavioral Therapy. Together, we decided in one particular session to try it.

She said, "Picture yourself in a safe place with the Lord, whatever that looks like for you. It can be real or imaginary."

A beautiful waterfall came to mind. I was sitting on a rock downstream. It felt indescribably peaceful.

Then she asked if Jesus could join me there. Unsure and hesitating a little, I decided it would be alright. His presence felt genuine. No words, just a tangible presence and peacefulness being there together.

As I described the picture to Laura, I realized Jesus wanted to tell me something, but I was afraid to hear it. He reassured me and spoke. He said, "The journey will be hard, but I will keep you safe. You will live and not die, but I need you to look at something with me."

I told Laura I didn't want to look, but she encouraged me. She asked, "What would help you to look?" I pictured myself in a high balcony, looking down on a stage with the curtains closed. Then, in my mind, I stacked a bunch of pillows all around me, with Jesus there beside me.

He said, "Are you ready to look?"

I said, "Do I have to?"

"Yes, you do," He replied. "Freedom will come as you face the truth."

Hopeful, I agreed that I would look. But first, I told Laura I had an overwhelming sense that I was going to die once I had seen what Jesus wanted to show me.

Laura prayed again and asked the Lord if there might be a dissociated part of me whose job it was to protect me from the memory and if not, would He reveal that.

I became like a little girl in the chair, hiding my face behind my hair, tears flowing.

Laura said, "How old do you feel?"

I sat frozen in fear, unable to speak.

"Are you afraid to speak?"

All I could do was nod my head, yes.

Then she asked the Lord when and where this part of me came into being.

Sobbing and hugging my knees, I still could not answer, even though I wanted to.

"How old do you feel?"

"Seven," came my sad whisper.

That was when I knew, and she knew, that this seven-year old was a part of me.

Laura said, "Lord, would you reveal the memory where this little seven-year-old came into being?

I went back to the balcony in my mind. Jesus opened the curtain and shined light on the stage.

Somehow, my dad had learned that my stepbrother had been sexually abusing me. He tried to kill both of us with a butcher knife. I hid under the kitchen table as he tried kicking me with the point of his cowboy boot, striking me in the jaw. In a panic, my mom ran into the room naked, trying to stop him, but she couldn't. I never understood why she was naked.

Miraculously, my grandfather arrived and physically restrained my father.

There is no fear like that kind of fear. That seven-year-old part of me had held all the fear and threat of death from the terror of that event.

Laura reassured me. "That was then, and this is now. You are safe here with me.

"Lord," she continued, "would you show her, where were You when it was happening?" The picture of Jesus protecting me from my dad came so clearly to my mind.

Then she asked Jesus, "Did she believe any lies about You, herself, or others when that happened to her? And if so, would You show her what they are?"

Barely audible, I got the words out: "I have to die. I'm worthless. I am not safe."

Next, Laura asked the Lord for truth to replace the lies. I had the specific impression that "I will live and not die and live more abundant and free," from John 10:10.

Laura had one more question though. "What job did that little seven-year-old take on, on the inside for the adult Sally?"

The job she'd been given was to kill me.

Laura asked that little seven-year-old part of me, "Would you be willing to release that job to Jesus and see what He would replace it with?"

I saw in my mind's eye a lush field of flowers next to the waterfalls. A little girl in a beautiful dress was there, freely dancing in pure joy. Instantly, I realized that if she would release the job to Jesus, she could be free to go and play.

Laura reassured her that she didn't have to give up the job, to give it to Jesus, if she didn't want to. She knew giving up the job of killing me was part of the little seven-year-old's identity. It was the very reason for her existence.

That part of me was hesitant at first, and a little fearful of Jesus. But as He approached her and knelt down, she ran into His arms and was so happy to be there.

"Healing! That's what true emotional healing is!" Laura exclaimed. "It's like that part of you will no longer need to exist apart from the rest of you. She can be integrated back into the rest of your mind after being broken off for all these years. It's emotional integration, which is our goal here."

She prayed that I could come back to an easy, gentle, normal state of being. She prayed some other things as well that I can't remember.

I do remember an overwhelming, tangible sense of relief. It was so powerful! It was true after all, and possible: genuine, miraculous, emotional healing.

What I had needed all along was a more powerful positive experience to replace the negative traumatic memory. Knowledge of the trauma had not been enough.

I was wiped out, wasted, but gradually came back around and had a sense of peace and freedom. Later, as I pondered the whole experience, I realized I had unconsciously lived with suicidal thoughts for as long as I could remember. Now, the thoughts could safely surface and be dealt with because of all the healing Jesus had provided.

I had never brought myself to the point of suicide because of the harm I knew it would cause my children. However, the temptation was serious enough that my first counselor had me sign a promissory note that I would not hurt myself.

Another odd thing: a couple of weeks before this breakthrough session, I'd had enough pain in my jaw to visit the dentist where she had diagnosed TMJ and fitted me with a night guard. I've since learned that we hold memories in our physical body.

I was certain that this memory was the root place I'd been trying to reach for the past ten years. That certainty gave me a sense of reassurance that it would all be over at last.

But no…

Making Sense of My World

I am paralyzed, frozen in fear, plagued by random thoughts… or is it voices? Is it possible that my reality is not reality? What will I do if I cannot trust my own mind? Where does that leave me?

An indescribable loneliness penetrated to the very core of my being. It was worse than isolation. It was worse than rejection. It was the dark night of the soul, plunging me back into dysfunctional depression.

The session with Laura where I first experienced the seven-year-old part of myself, and the tangible, emotional healing, did not counter the dissociation diagnosis. It was no longer a possibility, but a reality. And it sent me into despair.

At the same time, there was a sense of relief. Somebody finally knew and understood, even though I did not. Still trying to make sense of it all, I did the only thing I knew to do.

The internet wasn't as accessible as it is now, but I learned everything I could on dissociation. I read every book and attended every seminar that was even closely related to the topic. I have a tub full of notebooks and certifications from seminars and trainings I've attended over the last 25 years. I affectionately call it my LED: Life Experience Degree.

It's a complicated subject, but I was determined to make sense of it.

We have a variety of historical events in our life. These experiences make up our personality emotionally, physically, and spiritually. They also shape our emotional world and outward behavior. They make us who we are and craft how we think.

The tapestry of the current circuits in our brain are an accumulation of all the experiences we have had and the conclusions we have drawn about life. The good news is that our circuitry can be changed.

Safe, pleasant, fun, and loving events create normal, healthy neuropathways in the brain. Adverse experiences cause the circuits or neuropathways to be routed through the brain in abnormal ways, essentially causing damage to brain development. In many cases the adverse, traumatic, or stressful experiences are then buried from consciousness as a protective mechanism.

Although traumatic experiences or stress can cause damage to the neural pathways in the brain, God designed the brain to fragment, similar to a Ground Fault Circuit Interrupter (GFCI) built into an electrical outlet. These are designed to trip when a dangerous surge of electricity flows through a circuit. The GFCI prevents a dangerous overload of electricity from starting a fire or injuring someone. In the mind, this "trip," or fragmentation, helps children handle overwhelming emotions they just don't know what to do with—emotions that are beyond their capacity to process.

In the child's little mind, they can mentally and emotionally "fracture," which allows them to escape instead of being present and having to relive the pain of the trauma, especially if the trauma is recurring. If the trauma is acute, the initial reaction is to block it out and say this cannot be happening, pushing it away from their consciousness.

> "This process is a neural defense mechanism in the brain designed to protect the psyche of an individual from being incapacitated by fear-inducing memories." – Christopher Bergland, Psychology Today, "Unconscious Memories Hide In the Brain But Can Be Retrieved," August 17, 2015

As a result of this fragmentation, these memories are no longer consciously processed in the frontal lobe or active processing center of the brain but are stored in the subconscious brain. This gives the individual the capacity to survive and function. A type of amnesia is created, and the fear-related memories are inaccessible through normal cognition and consciousness.

This fracturing of the brain is called dissociation. Another way to look at it is that by fracturing or dissociating, the functioning "part" of a person is only an observer of the abuse occurring to a fractured "part" of the same person. This distancing is what enables a person to cope and survive.

The common medical term for this fracturing is Dissociative Identity Disorder (DID). To dissociate means to separate, detach, or disconnect. As Doug and Katie Merwin from Truth in Love Ministries state, "Dissociation is a normal, life-saving capability of the brain. It has been designed by God to protect us. It is not a disease or a mental illness."

Everyone dissociates to some degree, often without realizing it. To the extent that your brain is focused on something other than your present situation, you are dissociating.

The process of dissociating falls on a continuum. On the familiar, minor end, boredom or monotony can trigger a person to daydream, causing a person to miss a lesson in school, or forget the last twenty miles of a drive.

The other, more unfamiliar and difficult end of the spectrum is the creation of different "parts" or alternate personalities, where someone actually has "alters" and can unconsciously switch from one personality to another. This would be like what is shown in the movies Sybil or Split. Another example is The Victor Marx Story, which can be found on YouTube.

When you say, "I hate that part of myself," it can be literal. We all have wounded, child-like parts of ourselves who are trying to cope in a dysfunctional way in life. The part can be any age and can even be male or female, which is often the case with identity confusion. It can also be referred to as an "inner child" who is stuck emotionally at the age in which the trauma occurred. Thus, one sign of dissociation can be a person who exhibits behaviors inconsistent with the maturity expected from their chronological age.

Because that trauma is broken off, compartmentalized, and filed away unprocessed inside the brain, the child continues to live life out of the frontal lobe/front part of the brain so they can get up and function in their day-to-day activities as if nothing ever happened.

The problem is that the back of the brain is constantly living in this state of trauma, stuck at the age the person was traumatized.

> "Our capacity for freedom of choice and action is limited by our bondage to personality factors that operate beyond our awareness. In other words, it is that which we choose not to know or acknowledge about ourselves i.e. that which we repress, deny or in other ways relegate to the unconscious that has the most power over us … the more such things exist and the more unwilling we are to face them, the greater the bondage." Care of Souls, David Benner, page 161.

Again, everyone falls somewhere on the spectrum.

If you want a more technical explanation of how the brain processes trauma, you can research some of these Christian doctors who have expertise in this area.

Dr. Karl Lehman – Immanuel Ministries – has free articles online about pain-processing pathways.

Dr. Marcus Warner – Deeper Walk International – has a DID primer.

Dr. Jim Friesen

Dr. E. James Wilder

There are also more articles and information in the appendix.

I've worked with a lot of people on the subject of trauma. When I tell them what is actually going on, at first it's hard to get their head wrapped around it. But then it begins to resonate on the inside and they find relief because somebody finally understands them. I know that feeling very well.

The Marriage

A romantic attraction remains a complex mystery, which is what makes relationships such an exciting topic of conversation in every country and culture. People who wade into the marriage mystery learn many lessons over time. One lesson I learned is that we tend to marry our emotional equal.

In hindsight, after 50 years of marriage, I can see that our relationship was one where two very painful and unresolved childhoods collided in covenant.

Tom grew up in Columbus, Ohio. His painful story tragically begins on the first day of first grade, when his mother committed suicide. When he came home from school, the ambulance was taking her away. All at once, he lost his mother as well as the five basic needs of every human being: security, love, belonging, significance, and understanding. They left him and his younger sisters right along with their mother's body.

His dad married Genevieve with a new baby already in tow. At 19, Genevieve wasn't ready for the responsibility of one child, much less three stepchildren. She and her new husband, whom she called "Bugsy," spent their nights barhopping, neglecting the children. Tommy, at seven years old, became the caretaker of his younger sister Suzie as well as Judy, the toddler. His chaotic environment taught him a strategy for survival: grow up, take control, and get it done himself.

Going to school unfed and unkempt prompted authorities to remove the children from the home and charge Bugsy with child neglect and abuse. His choice was to go to jail or give up all parental rights. Tommy and Suzie went straight to an orphanage. The strict supervision there was a blessing in that it relieved Tommy of the adult responsibilities he was carrying. But the unemotional, uncaring, sterile circumstances closed his heart even further. No one knows what happened to Judy. Babies were often put up for adoption right away.

After a while, Tommy went into foster care, losing track of both sisters. At eight years old, he was adopted. The psychiatrist's interview of the parents-to-be concluded his adoptive mother had no business adopting children. The details of how his adoptive parents were able to sidestep the psychiatrist's recommendation is unclear, but the circumstances Tommy was thrown into only served to multiply the troubles of his heart.

The couple wouldn't adopt his sister Suzie because they had a fight on Thanksgiving Day when they brought both of them home for the day. Instead, they adopted another girl, which contributed to fracturing Tommy's heart even more.

When Tommy was in junior high, his adoptive father, Wendell, was in Germany as an Air Force chaplain. Tommy and his adoptive mother and sister moved to Gloversville, New York, with Grandma Goodie and Grandpa Art.

His adoptive mother was so controlling and anal, Tommy had to show her the toilet with his bowel movement every morning. She tried to make him wear dress shoes to school, but his best friend would bring him white tennis shoes to change into on the bus. He had a few ways of compensating for her control.

After Wendell's return from Germany, the family moved to Stewart Air Force base in Newburgh, New York. Leaving his grandparents was yet another loss.

An emotionally unavailable, controlling, mentally ill mother who controlled every move his father made as well, along with Tommy's history of neglect, led him down a rebellious path. He was compelled to endure counseling for his issues, but this did not change his behavior nor heal the wounds of his heart. When he cold-cocked his father out of deep anger, his parents enrolled him in a high school military academy. In retrospect, he believes this decision probably saved his life, and maybe theirs.

Tom was determined not to live at home after high school graduation. He and a friend had hitchhiked from New York to Colorado the summer before his senior year. The next summer they drove out to Colorado and enrolled in college at the small-town university where I lived.

Tom knew his parents would never pay for his college education. Out of sheer determination, he worked several jobs and secured student loans to survive. Once again, he was depending only on himself, getting things done. The 60's culture of marijuana, abusing alcohol, and free sex helped to numb the pain. Somehow, he managed to still do well in school.

***

Despite the pain and challenges facing us, God's sovereign hand orchestrated a unique introduction that blossomed into a marriage. Our relationship began when I accidently dialed a wrong phone number while attempting to call Bonnie, my high school girlfriend, who had an older brother who liked to play tricks on me.

"Is Bonnie there?"

"There's no Bonnie here."

"Come on, let me speak to your sister."

"But there's no Bonnie here, and I don't have a sister here anyway."

"Look, you are just trying to give me a hard time. Please, let me talk to her."

"Really, I don't know any Bonnie."

I paused. Maybe I have a wrong number, but I'm sure I dialed the right one.

"My name is Tom. What's your name?"

"Uhhh, Sally."

"Now do you believe me?"

"OK, I'm so sorry. I really thought you were Bonnie's big brother, just giving me a hard time."

By then we were laughing, so we kept talking. The conversation revealed that one of his friends was dating one of my friends. By the next weekend, our mutual friends had set us up for a blind date, which led to a rocky three-year courtship. Wounded souls and immaturity were left unchecked due to a lack of any real guidance on how to pursue a healthy courtship. As you can imagine, the drama of our relationship could inspire the script of any soap opera or reality TV show.

Tom agreed to work on the farm for my dad during the summer months, allowing us to see one another on a regular basis. A volatile week of interacting usually led to a Saturday night breakup, at which time I would demand that my father fire him. However, Tom was a good worker, and my dad valued his contribution over my fickle wishes. As a result, Tom would be in my life again come Monday morning. We were both back in the boat, trying to navigate the raging seas within us.

Tom was pursuing his business degree—a long way from the farm boys or cowboys that were my only other options. I knew I didn't have enough self-esteem or strength to leave home on my own. He asked me to marry him more than once, and I finally agreed.

When my dad wanted to know if I loved Tom, I replied, "What is love?" After all, it was the sixties. I said, "I just know he's a hard worker, good with money, and crazy about me." Also, he was from New York, so he was a worldly kind of guy. It seemed like enough at the time.

August 16, 1970, we held a church wedding with a simple reception afterwards. Receiving that much affection and attention from family and friends that day met a deep need in my heart, something I didn't know was possible. The wedding night seemed idyllic—marvelous actually—at the Hilton Inn in Denver. The shock came the second night of the honeymoon, when we moved to a ghetto motel with cigarette burns in the bedspread, the carpet too dirty to walk on. I tried not to notice.

Denver was our home for six months. Employment turned out to be temporary jobs so we moved back to the farm where Tom committed to work for my dad for one year. It felt like a waste of a college education, so in 1972 we moved to Colorado Springs. Mark, our son, was born in 1974, and our daughter, Mandy, in '77.

It was a promising life. We lived in a fun, child-filled neighborhood with lots of friends, and went on church campouts and vacations in the summer. All I had ever wanted was to be a wife and mother. In fact, I was Young Mother of the Year for the state of Colorado one year in the 80s.

Tom's priorities turned to work, playing in his baseball league, watching any seasonal sport on TV, and working out. Being the good provider, he worked hard. However, it did seem to be his life we were living. I just went along with my head down, trying to make life work by people-pleasing out of the same fear I had been raised in. I stuffed all the pain I had brought into the marriage with me, because that's what a good, submissive, Christian wife and mother should do.

Helen Reddy's song, "You and Me Against the World," haunted my soul, expressing the isolation and loneliness I felt in caring for the children and in the marriage. Tom's parenting style seemed oppressive and abusive to me, so I would try to protect the children from his harshness to keep the peace. I never even mentioned that I might have needs, partly because I was unaware of them myself. It never occurred to me those emotions could be rooted in my childhood and reinforced by the present circumstances.

Every week, the groceries cost too much for Tom, the kid's needs cost too much, and eating out not even an option. Leaving lights on or turning up the heat was a criminal offense. After at least ten years of scrounging out of the change jar to buy a soda or let the kids go to the 7-11, I begged for a five-dollar weekly allowance. Anything I bought had to be justified, but there always seemed to be money for fishing trips, major league games, or going to Las Vegas with the guys.

My role consisted of having dinner on the table at 5:30 pm every night, keeping the groceries stocked, doing the laundry, cleaning the house, and raising the children. As long as I kept up my side of the bargain, it would all work out, I was sure. But I never knew when or what was going to set off Tom's anger. Looking back, I can now see that each beer added to the equation and escalated the hostility of our interactions.

As I entered my thirties, I sought to gauge what a "normal" marriage relationship looked like by questioning my friends. My own parents and grandparents hadn't provided a proper frame of reference for how to do life any differently. I had no idea at the time that the traumatic experiences of my childhood were anything but normal. Perhaps I didn't know the right questions to ask, for it seemed as though my friends' experiences were too different from mine to be attainable.

As the years passed, I began to see more clearly just how demeaning Tom's treatment toward me was at the time, and how his strategy to do life bled into the marriage. Yet, he too lacked any real modeling on how to do better. Nonetheless, being treated like a child who is unable to do anything right contributed to the further erosion of how I viewed my own value and worth. I didn't even know at the time that being demeaned is a form of control.

As I've mentioned, we all adopt strategies for living, and Tom had chosen control. So the man who I saw as "good with money" used anger to keep finances in balance and fear at bay. Our finances matched his values, not mine. When I finally figured out his paycheck wasn't "our" money, I started cleaning house for a friend and babysitting in order to stay at home with the kids. This also allowed me to have a little money that didn't require me to justify exactly how it was spent.

The knight in shining armor who rescued me from the farm turned out to be just another dictator in my mind. The same atmosphere I grew up in after all. There I was again, being dehumanized under an abusive, authoritarian attitude, held accountable for every dollar, living in fear of not only disapproval and rejection but harm.

Despite the difficulties in our marriage, I am thankful for the opportunity I was afforded by Tom's professional stability to stay home for ten years with the children. As the kids got older, I realized having my own money was a key to my survival and decided to get back into the marketplace. Plus, Tom pressured me to do so.

I started with temporary jobs, then finally began working full-time. Work provided an outlet for me to begin finding a new identity. I was appreciated and complimented for my performance on the job. I also finally had money that I was free to spend in alignment with who I am and what I value. In my mind, I was certain this was the answer I had been looking for, the one that would solve all of our problems. For the first time, I felt empowered, like I was in the driver's seat. I bought beautiful clothes and jewelry and decorated the house—things I had always wanted.

At the height of this season, I even went on a trip to Mexico with girlfriends and had fun, something that I had forgotten was a possibility. This trip created the space I needed to take a deep breath, which I had held for a long time. Unfortunately, as I boarded the plane to return, I immediately felt suffocated by the thought of going home. The tears never stopped during that flight and they revealed the depth of my misery and desperation.

The Dance

It's called "the dance." Two people are in relationship. When one changes, the other one either changes too, or moves away from the partner.

He moved away.

Not that I could blame him.

Growing through counseling meant life or death for me. Coming out of the depression seemed like a healthy trajectory. However, since the root of depression is anger turned inward, my rage gradually turned outward and needed a place to vent along the way.

Ten years of good Christian counseling gave me enough self to express my anger. After twenty-five years of acquiescing and suppressing animosity, I erupted, and the marriage finally unraveled.

There was so much hostility and friction in the room, even opening the windows didn't help. The conflicts were excruciating, but I was finally able to begin letting the anger out. My counselor suggested doing something harmless to express it. Throwing empty plastic milk jugs at the solid wood back door seemed harmless enough. I threw harder and harder each time, only realizing later that I had put dents in the door. Another time, I beat all the shirts off Tom's hangers with a belt.

But at the lowest moment, during one interaction in our driveway, the seething hatred and disgust created enough spit in my mouth to land in his face. It almost felt demonic because the side effects of my anti-depressant gave me dry mouth. Stunned, I had no idea I was capable of that.

Finally, I burned all but one of the wedding pictures. I had not a drop of hope left.

Neither one of us wanted divorce, but we separated for the first time in 1992, for six months.

Separating broke my heart for our kids, but at the same time, it helped me realize that I had been miserable for a very long time.

Pain piled on top of pain. The rejection I felt created a chasm in my heart…a break that seemed irreparable. It was as per-manent, I thought, as the Grand Canyon.

During this time, I painted my first oil painting and named it "The Dark Night of the Soul." It's very dark and somber but has this little place of yellow-gold in the middle. Some-where inside, I knew that gold represented life. It gave me a way to physically express what I could not put into words.

I increased my sessions to twice a week, every week. In addi-tion to my Inner Healing Prayer sessions with more horrific memories surfacing, I started meeting with another coun-selor—a gentle and kind Mennonite man—for my marriage. He helped me navigate the separation/conflict maze.

"Sally, Tom's a steam roller. He just rolls right over you and leaves you lying in the ditch," he said.

It was the first time someone really reflected my experience.

In my mind, it was the miserable muck of a marriage and he, a dictator. We simply could not relate in a meaningful, compassionate, or healthy way.

After the first separation, Tom and I reunited, but it was mostly because of the children and the holidays. Still in conflict but trying our best to work it out, we only lasted three years.

Here we were, going to the children, breaking hard news to them yet again. Mark attended college in another state, and Mandy was living with a widow and her daughter from our church.

Our pastor counseled Tom to file for a divorce, and most of our friends moved in Tom's direction. One of the wives that I thought was my friend worked as a bank teller at our bank. She started avoiding me every time I went in.

Tom bought himself a house, and I was "allowed" to stay in our family home. We looked into a legal separation, and reality set in for him. He realized I was entitled to fifty per cent of everything. With a government retirement plan in place, Tom felt the pain. After six months of separation, he reconsidered and moved back home with me.

The poor children…indescribable heartbreak came over me each time, knowing how shattered they were, yet I was unable to "do" the marriage even for their sake.

Suicide rose up like a geyser. The temptation intensified every time I closed the garage door. Overcome with hopelessness, bombarded with messages from the past, most sane thoughts out of reach, there was only one thing preventing me: knowing the harm my suicide would cause for the children saved my life again and again.

Three years later, in 1998, came separation number three. This had to be it. I was done. I got the best lawyer, referred by my church, but he was mostly after my money, and a little flirty for an old man.

The next lawyer was a better fit, so I promptly filed for divorce. We managed to buy a decent townhome for me, and Tom kept our home: "our home," the place filled with so many family gatherings and other wonderful memories. To be excluded from what would go on there seemed truly unbearable. Imagining another woman in my house left me without words, but there was nothing I could do.

There were no wedding pictures left to burn or I would have. It was symbolic of just how done I was with the relationship.

How much more, Lord?

I can't go on.

I just can't.

You have forgotten me!

The most vivid memory I have of that time is being on my knees, face down, listening to worship music, sobbing. It was all I could do. The pain had to come out. I couldn't pray or read my Bible. Nothing consoled me. I only thought I was in too much pain before, but I knew God was all I had left. I would tell Him I had more tears in a bottle than anyone else.

Other men started calling, asking me out and showing up at my door. That really came as a surprise. Somehow God protected me, and I knew I didn't have the capacity to even go there—not to mention that I was still married.

Tom seemed to have women around all the time, keeping them in his back pocket like a "Plan B." It leaked out in our conversations when we would meet to "do business," which were our attempts to work out most of the divorce details ourselves.

My daughter came over one day and encouraged me to complete the divorce. Hearing that from my own child helped me realize we had all been through enough.

Tom conveniently left for the NASCAR races in Ohio when it was time for me to move to the townhouse. He left me without any help, so I took everything I wanted from our family home.

Working to support myself now, for the first time I had all the responsibilities of home ownership, the car, and the finances. Not once in the marriage had I paid a bill or known the balances in the bank accounts. It was a growing experience and very good for me in the end. I needed to learn that I could be an independent adult and provide for myself, growing my self-confidence from zero to something more.

Despite all the support for the seemingly inevitable divorce, there were moments that gave me pause.

One day my four-year-old grandson was visiting me and the sweet little guy said, "Nana, why do you live in town and Papa lives at your house?"

"Well, I guess we needed a timeout." I replied. Apparently, three timeouts.

My two best friends were divorced, and they encouraged me to do everything I could to work things out with Tom. How they described the afterlife in detail helped me significantly. Every family gathering would be uncomfortable for the rest of our lives. And where would I go when the children and grandchildren were with Tom for Thanksgiving or Christmas or birthdays? The thought was agonizing. Those conversations gave me a true reality check.

And then, since it was our anniversary, I agreed to take a drive to the mountains with Tom. My body language said it all: I was physically plastered to the passenger door, revealing how unsafe I felt in his presence.

I explained to him what my friends were telling me about the reality of the "afterlife." Barely able to contain myself, I pummeled him with questions:

"You know the money has to stretch a lot further after you pay me my half."

"Do you spend Christmas with her kids or your kids? You will have to buy presents for them as well as your own kids and grandkids?" (His Plan B at this point had younger children.)

"Do you go to her kid's events or your grandkid's events if there's a conflict?"

"Are you going to help pay for their college?"

"Will you bring someone else to our family gatherings or come by yourself?"

"By the way, I will be there too—maybe with somebody else, maybe not."

His response was stone silence for the whole trip.

Shortly after that ride to the mountains, Tom started asking me to come back home. At first, I replied with a few choice words I don't normally use. Then the Lord began to work on me. I knew I should go back, but it felt like there was no way in hell that I could.

Through one of my counselors, I learned of a marriage ministry in town that held weeklong intensives for couples in crisis. I told Tom that if he would go, I would come back home. He refused, right up to the night before.

I finally said, "Well, I will be there at 8:30 am. If you are, fine. If you are not, fine."

He showed up.

It's a grueling week. The first assignment was to write down all the ways we'd been hurt in the relationship. I listed twenty-some items. Tom's list had four items. Next, we were to ask each other for forgiveness. I asked for his forgiveness freely and sincerely. He refused to ask for mine. It crushed me.

That night, I called the counselor and said, "I cannot continue the rest of the week."

The power in what our counselor did stunned me. He said, "Sally, will you forgive me for every way your husband has hurt you?"

Melting into the floor, undone and sobbing for several minutes, I barely managed to get out, Yes.

It is hard to describe the release that came over me by that man standing in place of Tom and asking for my forgiveness. It is what Jesus did on the cross for us. He stood in our place so that we are forgiven for all of our sin. The presence of the Lord Jesus in that moment was palpable, changing my heart.

I went back for the counseling intensive the next day, freed from the hurt, bitterness, and resentment that represented my side of the wall between us.

The week-long intensive gave us a place to begin working through most of the issues between us, but more importantly, it taught us to hear each other's hearts. It was a monumental difference from only hearing each other's words. It was kindergarten communication, but we could hear each other for the first time in a very long time. We learned compassion for each other's childhood woundings, and we discovered each other's triggers that caused our overreactions. This taught us how to resolve our own unique conflicts. Who knew that was possible?

Tom agreed to see the Mennonite counselor with me a few times. That helped us work through our major issues. Then, suddenly, Tom informed me that he and a friend were coming to the townhome with a moving van to carry my things "home."

In very little faith, I did it. I believe I left heel marks in the pavement all the way home.

Nothing More Evil

After the third and final reconciliation with my husband, I opened the door to optimism, believing there was room for it in my heart. After all, shouldn't fifteen years of counseling and reaching the half-century mark in birthdays be rewarded with total recovery?

Following the zig-zag line of my depression highs and lows helped put things in perspective. During the early cycles, I would be very low and stay down for long periods of time. However, as the years and healing progressed, I could see that both the depth and length of time I stayed under became less and less. A little counseling nugget like that revealed momentum and provided motivation for continued perseverance.

After a while, though, reality proved that total recovery may not be achievable. I was better, but not truly well. I had a lingering sense of oppression—like that one extended family member that nobody likes, but everyone tolerates because they have to. I would go along well for a while, until a mistake or a conflict would shut me down and I'd end up in bed again.

There's something fundamentally wrong with me. That was the biggest lie circulating in my brain. I had done everything

I possibly knew to do to get well. Whoops! There it is—always trying to fix myself with what I "do." I belong to the performance-based, perfection-based people group. It's my default strategy.

I believed my identity and safety depended on "doing it right." When I couldn't maintain doing right, the confusion and crash began.

My mind knew God loved me unconditionally, but my heart still believed if I didn't mess up too bad, just prayed and read my Bible more, life might be better. Actually it came down to the idea that "If I do this, then God will do that." Heavenly quid pro quo at its finest.

Truth be told, I simply was worn out trying.

The Inner Healing Prayer sessions taught me to feel safe with Jesus within those settings, but the safety didn't transfer to my personal time alone with Him. I usually felt disconnected and lost from God. If you asked me, I would present a picture that I knew my experience betrayed. I truly did love Him, but I just felt empty inside and alone. Other people seemed to genuinely experience His presence. From what I gathered, His presence seemed to come during times of stillness and solitude, but these activities left me uneasy and never lasted more than a few seconds. I only felt safe when I prayed "at" Him or read something "about" Him, because I projected the horrible punishment from my father onto God. How could anyone relate to that kind of God?

Even church was uncomfortable. Sermons were hard to remember after I left the sanctuary. Altar prayers didn't seem to change much for me as they appeared to for others. Small group circles left me feeling awkward and barely able to speak up.

I hated being the center of attention, yet always feeling like someone was watching. Part of my strategy to keep myself safe depended on never being the focus of attention.

The depth of grief that hovered close to the surface felt like a dear friend waiting to comfort me but unable to get close enough to do so. Tears came easily.

***

Disclaimer:

One, I would be glad to deny the following if it hadn't happened to me.

Two, I would never have believed it from someone else.

Here I am again, dragging myself to what seems like my five-hundredth counseling appointment. Katie warmly welcomed me into the safest place I knew, her office. Her welcome gradually replaced one of my greatest fears, arising from my attachment disorder: the fear of not being welcome in this life.

I unloaded before she asked a question.

"My husband said we could go for separation number four then claimed to be just kidding. I've been numb ever since... can't eat, can't sleep, can't talk...shut down. Why? He was just kidding. Please don't remind me that my reaction should be equal to the event. I know I'm overreacting." I felt my lips quivering, sobs taking over. "I automatically go to the worst-case scenario. What is wrong with me?"

In her wise counselor way, she empathized with her own tears. She saw the pain and heard the cry coming from a deep place inside me. "Of course that would be triggering. Let's ask Jesus to take this current event to the very root place it might be coming from—to the first time you felt abandonment—and reveal why it's so triggering."

In prayer, she asked Jesus to go to that part of the brain that might hold a memory where I first believed I could never be left alone.

The image that came to mind had me looking down from above the clouds, through a portal in the sky. A river near our town, with a grove of trees and a dozen 1950's cars parked nearby, came sharply into my awareness. I then saw my parents and older brother, their backs toward me. They were walking away, leaving me out there alone. Why?

She could tell I was shaken to my core by the image. "What do you need?" she asked. I let out a soft, deep cry, bordering on a scream of pain. Then she said, "Can I ask Jesus where He was and how He was feeling when that happened to you?" Barely able to nod a yes and never looking up, I became like that little three-year old, shaking uncontrollably in my chair.

Jesus came into the picture, but I was afraid of Him. I didn't want to go near Him. How could I know He was safe?

"What do you need to feel safe with Him?" she asked.

"Will He hurt me?" I said in a very childlike voice.

"Let's ask Him," she said.

He began to cry.

In disbelief, I whispered, "Does Jesus cry?"

"Yes, that's how you can know it's the True Lord Jesus. It broke His heart that they did that to you."

Then I saw Him kneel and open His arms to welcome me. I ran into them, feeling the most gentle love and compassion I had ever known...making Him completely safe. He spoke into my spirit. "I will never leave you or forsake you." This was the truth my inner child needed to hear in the place she needed to hear it...not intellectually, but emotionally.

Katie said, "A lie believed in the heart is more powerful than the truth believed in the mind." Then she asked Jesus what lies I was believing about myself, God, or others when that happened to me at the river. I distinctly heard:

I am all alone.

I am worthless.

I'm not worth loving.

I'm not worth being cared for.

I'm not safe anywhere.

I don't belong in this world.

"Would you be willing to break those lies by repeating a prayer after me?"

I agreed. (This prayer is included in the appendices.)

"I would like to ask Him one more thing if that's alright with you."

I nodded, still unable to speak.

"Jesus, what job did this little three-year-old do for the adult Sally? What is her job on the inside?"

Aware that the silent scream meant this part of me held all the pain from the abandonment and the recurring consequences, I knew it was this three-year-old's job to keep all that pain hidden and under control. Finally, I said, "I just need to let the scream out."

Because there were others in the building, she suggested I stand in the closet with a pillow over my mouth, shut the door, and let it out.

Out came all the piercing pain, in a scream that lasted for what seemed like ten long minutes. Finally, I collapsed on the floor. A visceral relief spread through me.

When I recovered, she asked Jesus for the truth to replace the lies I had come to believe. In my spirit, I heard:

I will never leave you or forsake you.

You are worth dying for.

I love you with an everlasting and unconditional love.

You are more precious than gold.

I will keep you safe, and you belong with Me.

Then Katie said, "Jesus, would you give her a word picture for all the pain she is holding?"

A visual of a backpack filled with huge rocks came to my mind, the three-year old crawling on hands and knees under its crushing weight. Trying to do life with this backpack of rocks was like climbing a gigantic mountain at the same time.

"Would you be willing to give that backpack of rocks to Jesus and see what He would like to replace it with?"

Nodding in agreement, I saw Him take each rock out, one by one, and lay them at the foot of the cross. In my spirit I knew that every rock represented a time I had experienced abuse. As soon as it was laid at the cross, each rock instantly turned to gold dust.

When He finished, I ran over and started throwing the gold dust up in the air with Him, laughing. Only later would I realize the gold dust represented how much He valued my suffering.

***

Katie and I took a break to rest. When we started back up, she asked me if I had enough energy for one more question.

She suggested there might need to be some reconciliation with the adult Sally on the inside. That just sounded weird to me. But, again, I trusted her and the process.

"Go back and picture the little three-year-old there with Jesus. Then could we invite the adult Sally to join them?" Hesitant but willing, in my mind's eye I saw a little girl, the adult me, and Jesus there together.

"What does the little one need from the adult Sally?"

In that moment, I recognized she needed the adult Sally to take care of her. She had been taking care of the adult Sally by holding all the pain of the abandonment. Now, she wanted the freedom to be a child.

I watched the video play out in my mind as the adult Sally told the little one, "I am an adult now. I can take care of myself and you." The child hugged the adult with relief and love. Then the little one, the adult, and Jesus walked away.

Miraculously, in the same way I'd watched my parents and brother walk away.

Leaving Katie's office that day, the world seemed lighter and brighter—because I was lighter and brighter on the inside. I had emotional eyes to see my world differently. I knew there was more work to do, but that day became a marker for hope.

I share all of this only to expose that what the enemy intends for evil, God can use for good.

Over the next few years, a series of memories revealed that when I was two years old, my parents began handing me over to a masonic satanic cult—mostly on weekends. Rituals were outdoors in summer and in the basement of our church in winter. There I would be on Sunday mornings, watching these men worship God, when the night before they'd ritually abused me.

I've chosen not to share all that was done to me during that two- or three-year period. But for the sake of revealing the atrocities that occur to mostly children, even today, I will share one. You would be surprised to find out how much still goes on today. Please skip it if you feel uncomfortable.

Satanic cults often use a "jesus" mask to speak pronouncements and lies over children during the rituals (I am intentionally using a lowercase j here because this is a false jesus).

This particular counseling session revealed a memory where I was buried alive in a coffin. Someone behind a jesus mask put me in the coffin, while speaking a pronouncement over and over, "You cannot have the Breath of Life."

Jesus is the Breath of Life.

Dirt falling on the wooden boards of the coffin instilled the ultimate horror. Shaking uncontrollably and silently weeping, I had no voice to express my terror.

There were holes drilled in the coffin so my little four-year-old self would live and come out believing that I could not breathe and have Jesus at the same time.

This is how programming works, causing just enough pain for the child to dissociate, then implanting falsehoods. Brainwashing on steroids.

At the same time, dissociation is a gift from God for children to be able to leave their bodies and watch what is happening so they don't have to fully experience the trauma.

The Healing Prayer session around this memory was very similar to the abandonment one. Each session would reveal a child (dissociated part) who held the memory, while having a job on the inside. The jobs were different, like keeping me (the adult) safe, or having responsibility for the other parts on the inside, or protecting that part from going to the trauma memory. Each little one would also have lies they were believing, inner vows they may have made, and more. My counselor used a repertoire of prayers for breaking lies, pronouncements, vows, seals, covenants, and agreements the ritual abusers used to further the secrecy around their rituals. The main prayer is posted in the Appendix.

As I've shared, though I became an adult on the outside, I lived this child's life of paranoia and unbridled fear on the inside.

The brain operates in daily life out of the frontal lobe so that you are able to function. All the trauma is blocked off into the cerebral cortex at the back of the brain, but it's constantly scrambling to keep everything operational. (There is plenty of brain science out there to research if you want further understanding.)

Hyperventilating, panic attacks, nightmares, and insomnia became common occurrences for me. I've tried to describe before how much constant fear I lived with. Every scenario, thought, and action was based on keeping myself safe. The energy consumption proved debilitating, which led to my depression.

Satanic Ritual Abuse (SRA) has been performed by organizations that have existed for centuries, causing generation after generation to be abused and broken. Cult abuse is too complicated to fully cover here. Basically, though, cults use premeditated strategies of inflicting pain in order to bring the mind into a dissociative state. Dissociation, as I've previously discussed, is the separation of an idea or event from one's mainstream of consciousness. It serves as a protection or defense mechanism.

For some, the pain inflicted is so great, the part of the brain processing the trauma dissociates and becomes compartmentalized as an alter/personality. This isolated part is then systematically programmed with lies and distortions to bring about satan's agenda on the earth: structured mind control (I intentionally use a lowercase s because the enemy deserves no honor). The falsehoods are the exact opposite of biblical truths, even presenting a false jesus and using Bible verses to speak the perversions.

This calculated process "creates" a system of family alters, also called parts or personalities with specific jobs. The complexity varies, depending on the amount of exposure to traumatic experiences. The cult's purpose is to rewire the brain—the wonderful brain God created with all its magnificence—by constructing a pattern of thinking that will serve darkness. Because we are physical, emotional, and spiritual beings, the abusers intentionally move through physical, emotional, and spiritual levels.

The mission of the cult is to deliberately bring about destruction and loose every evil in the world. Each alter seeks to function in the world despite being equipped only with unconscious, faulty strategies. Their attempts at living life are thwarted by events that trigger them to react in various ways in order to take control of a situation and keep the system "safe."

One way I used to keep my system safe was to take control anytime I perceived danger or a situation getting out of control. Not knowing, I would immediately dissociate and be impartial around a crisis as it was happening. It's very common for survivors to be controlling personality types, great in a crisis with the ability to remain completely calm.

A feeling of being "stuck" in a situation is common, also. By that I mean that I wanted to change what I was saying or how I was acting but couldn't. I felt confined in my mind or in my body. If I was stuck in a child-like part that was very young, I wouldn't have the words or vocabulary to respond.

Ritual abuse needs to be exposed. Why isn't it? Cults use power and control through the rituals, insuring secrecy. Otherwise, the path would lead directly to themselves.

This is the greatest evil perpetrated on mankind which mankind tends to deny exists.

There is nothing more evil. It's almost beyond human understanding except that humans abuse fellow humans with a dissociative indifference every day.

And like I said, if it hadn't happened to me, I would never believe it.

***

Here was the root cause at last. It explained why I was the way I was. Why I had struggled for so long. Why I never knew I had core longings that were not only never met, but how I had been programmed to believe the opposite of the truth that I am significant. I have purpose. I am secure. I belong and I am loved. Lie after lie had left me handicapped to do life in any sort of meaningful way.

The abandonment by my own parents and the ritual programming required extra Inner Healing Prayer sessions for several more years. One session revealed that my being sold to the cult had provided food for our family. Somehow it lessened the betrayal, since it had met our tangible needs.

Though I was definitely relieved to know the truth at last, I was still devastated. I didn't share any of my sessions with anyone else for a long time. It really messed with me. I would come home so incapacitated from my sessions, it forced me to let my husband know bits and pieces, but only the bare minimum.

I could never leave my mind. There was no escape.

A basic trust of the inner healing process, measurable recovery, the gift of perseverance, and knowing the Lord was intimately involved, prevented me from killing myself while giving me glimpses of wholeness. I'd come a long way from seeing no light at the end of the tunnel and planning to leave the car running in the garage.

I believe most mental illness and dysfunction is when a person cannot process something traumatic that happened to them. Not everyone's mental illness is caused specifically by this, but I do wonder if this is true for more people than we think.

Like I said from the beginning, I should be in a mental hospital or dead.

***

I remember during an earlier part of my journey, my parents had come for one of their annual visits. After a long day walking around the flea market, my dad said, "Sally, I need you to forgive me for something."

Thinking he meant the physical and emotional abuse, and too uncomfortable to discuss it, I cut him off.

"That's okay," I said. "I've already forgiven you."

At that point, I had not yet remembered the sexual and ritual abuse. Now that he's passed, I often wonder what he wanted to ask me that day.

Out of my increasing wholeness, love and forgiveness grew in my heart: love because I drew closer to Jesus; forgiveness because I understood that what was done to me had been done to them. In my parents' final days on earth, I genuinely loved them both.

God restored what was severely broken in my life through counseling and Inner Healing Prayer. Revealing the enemy's plans and schemes meant getting some revenge for what was done to me. It's the only time revenge is healthy! I also formed an Inner Healing Prayer Ministry called His Gathering, to help others go after the enemy's jugular as they move forward in their journey toward emotional freedom.

Triggers

Emotions. Can you trust them?

Well, not totally. They are there for a reason though. God created us with emotions. They are a gift. Neither right nor wrong they just are. We feel what we feel. Emotions are telling us something about our inner world.

As a child, I was beaten for getting in trouble, then beaten for crying about being beaten. I learned to bury most of the painful emotions around the severe sexual, physical, emotional, and spiritual abuse. As a result, I lived a life of chronic despair, hopelessness, and depression.

The fear of shame, and of more pain and rejection kept me walled off, isolated, in bondage.

That is how, by 35 years old, I had become a dormant volcano on the verge of erupting.

While silence appeared to be a pathway to safety, it is in fact an invitation to a slow death. The pain eats away at an individual's emotional, spiritual, and physical well-being like a cancer.

The lie I believed all those years is, "If I go there, I will die." There is the trauma of childhood with the attached psychological damage. The truth I learned is, "If I go there, I will live and live more, abundant and free."

The repression is costly. The dilemma as an adult becomes the triggers that set off the emotional reactions.

Trigger, the verb, is to cause (an event or situation) to happen or exist.

Emotional trigger, the noun, is something that puts you in a state of being unable to respond rationally.

Being triggered is the worst feeling. Rationally, you know what you should do, but an internal force takes over, and you cannot bring yourself to do it. You are in the flight or fight part of the brain instead of your frontal lobe where you can reasonably navigate your circumstances.

Why are we plagued by triggers? In short: because we were all children once. When we were growing up, we inevitably experienced pain or suffering that we could not acknowledge or deal with sufficiently at the time. So as adults, we typically become triggered by experiences that are reminiscent of historically painful feelings. As a result, a habitual or addictive way of trying to manage the painful feelings is set in motion.

Trying to manage my emotions without realizing there were triggers left me in a chaotic state of confusion. Different parts of myself were triggered by different situations, forcing me to be on guard at all times. The trigger could be a sight, a sound, a smell, or any situation or comment. A lifetime of post-traumatic stress disorder.

The rejection from our three marital separations was a major trigger. I overreacted each time in different ways—the obvious one being filing for divorce when I did not believe in it. Spitting in his face also might be considered an overreaction. It was the weirdest feeling. I felt overtaken by a force, even though I knew it would be wrong. I had no idea it was a dissociative part of me that took over.

Rarely now, but occasionally, I still find myself in that state.

One Thanksgiving, my sister-in-law asked me to leave a setting empty at the table for her five-year-old to set up his coloring cloth. I forgot to do it. The minute she walked in the door, she began yelling at me in front of the other guests while I raced over to the table and cleared it off. I shut down. Fuming on the inside, I could not look at her or talk to her throughout the whole dinner. All that time, I was trying to talk myself out of my stupor, but couldn't. That's when I knew I was overreacting out of a child-like part. My next session with Katie went something like this:

Me: "I just feel like I can never do it right."

Katie: "How old do you feel?"

Four clearly came into my mind.

Katie: "Let's ask the Lord if He wants to show you where that might be coming from. Jesus, would you go to the very root place where she may have come to believe the lie that she can 'never do it right'?"

A long silence followed. I waited as a video of growing up crossed my mind, a pattern. I described what I saw to Katie.

Me: "There is a pattern beginning in the ritual abuse. I'm being forced into a lose-lose scenario. Sometimes having to watch others be tortured, then be programmed to believe it was my job to save them. I was too little to help in any way."

Katie confirmed that this was accurate, she being a ritual abuse survivor herself. Ritual abusers often use that scenario in order to bring about an incapacity to cope in adult life.

Katie said, "This is called a double-bind, and it's used often by the abusers." She turned to pray. "Jesus, what did four-year-old Sally come to believe in that place about herself, You, or others?"

As I listened, I felt His answers and spoke them aloud. I said, "I have to be perfect. And if I do it wrong, I will get hurt. It's my job to keep everyone safe." That last one would require another session. "I'm damned if I do, and damned if I don't."

Katie and I broke the lies together in prayer. Katie said, "Jesus, would you speak truth to the innermost parts?"

I felt Him speaking and spoke His words aloud. "I am human. He loves me whether I do it right or wrong."

With Katie's guidance, that little child part gave the job of having to "do it right" back to Jesus and integrated into the adult.

***

On another occasion, my husband and I planned to visit my 93-year-old mother on our trip to Arizona. She'd gone from assisted living to the hospital with a severe uterine infection and was then released to a nursing home. As we left her and headed on down the road, I poured my heart out to my husband through tears for what seemed like ten minutes.

"I'm afraid I'll never see her again. What if she dies while we are in Arizona? How would I get back in time to say good-bye?"

He turned to me in the car and said, "What did you say?"

I lost it. I was livid. He'd forgotten his hearing aids. I refused to speak to him for the rest of the eight-hour drive. In my mind, if you love someone, you want to hear them. Was that an overreaction? I think so, with a few drops of stubborn. I just could not pull myself out of the shutdown. I went into that child part that felt unheard and hopeless.

Of course, in my next counseling session this was the event to pray through. In the memory, Jesus showed me another pattern—not being heard growing up. The lies I believed were "I am not worth listening to." And "I have no voice." I broke the lies in prayer and heard Him speak into my spirit, "I always want to hear what you have to say." And, "Anything you say is important to me."

Another trigger for me is when someone leaves me, or if I fear that they will. I feel helpless in the midst of that pain.

My adult married children have had very difficult situations with some of their children—my grandchildren. In different ways, I have received the message that they didn't want to hear anything I might suggest. Because my life's work centers around emotional healing and understanding why people do what they do, feeling discounted was especially painful. Pain emanated mostly from watching everyone suffer—sometimes needlessly. Also, from not being heard and valued, as well as being rejected and dishonored.

As Katie prayed with me in one particular session, the Lord revealed that my hurt came from the memory of being responsible for my four younger brothers growing up. I took in those lies from eight years old onward. I was constantly overwhelmed as a young child with the responsibility of caring for younger siblings.

The lies I came to believe in that memory:

- I am responsible for everyone.

- I should have/could have done something.

- I must have done it wrong.

- Nobody cares.

- I have to fix people.

Katie asked the Lord for the truth. I clearly heard:

"You are full of love and compassion—that's all that's wrong with you, my daughter. You love well. But when you love well, it can be very hurtful. People will reject you, misunderstand you as they did Me. Thank you for loving so much that you are acquainted with My suffering. You see My grief because they could not hear Me either. They could not understand that what I had for them was so much better. A better way. Welcome to My world."

Another lie that came out later: when people reject my ideas, there is no place to take my pain. Jesus tenderly showed me that He has taken the pain in my place and can hold it for me.

The night of that session, as I listened to instrumental music to fall asleep, I clearly heard Him say, "I love your children, and I hold each one in the palm of My hand." Waking in the morning, I had peace and joy.

Subsequently, He taught me the difference between helping and rescuing. Helping means to come alongside, to support, aid, or assist versus saving from danger, harm, or evil. Did I mention the word savior? The ritual abuse programming that told me I have to save everybody, and a life of overwhelming responsibility for my siblings both contributed to my seeing myself as a savior.

The truth He taught me in that season: He is the One and only rescuer and Savior in life.

Here are a few more ways I suffered from being triggered over and over, whether it was intentional on a person's part or not:

- Someone ignoring me.

- Someone being unavailable to me.

- Someone giving me a disapproving look.

- Someone blaming or shaming me.

- Someone being judgmental or critical.

- Someone being too busy to make time for me.

- Someone not appearing to be happy with me or to see me.

- Someone trying to control me.

The trigger would cause me desolation to the point of numbing out, unable to cope or function normally. Only after an Inner Healing Prayer session would I be able to stabilize.

Just a reminder that whenever a person's response is not equal to the event—they overreact or underreact—you can be sure it is coming from their history.

For example, why would a 69-year-old man lie down in front of his truck so it wouldn't be towed away because the IRS was seizing it? True story.

The officer says, "You're acting like a three-year-old."

The man says, "I feel like a three-year-old."

That three-year-old part of him is who is actually responding to the event. The three-year-old part of him was being triggered by helplessness that catapulted him into that childlike part of his psyche. That three-year-old part of him took over, then laid down and threw a fit.

Triggers can be our friend, but only if we embrace what happens and seek understanding. Awareness is crucial. I have to check in with myself and ask the hard questions.

"Was that an overreaction or underreaction?"

"Was my response appropriate to the event?"

"Does it cause me to go to a place of desolation, confusion or feeling stuck, in a place I don't want to be?"

It was a long time before I could do that in the moment though. Now, I can cry out to the Lord and wait on His voice or go to a safe person and describe what was happening on the inside. I've included an exercise in the appendix called "STOP" that will help with the spiral down.

The simplest method to be released from a trigger in the moment is to repeat over and over, "That was then and this is now."

Wholeness

"Wholeness does not mean perfection.

Wholeness means embracing imperfection.

We are both darkness and light." Parker Palmer

When I use the word wholeness, I mean a state of being that is an internal unifying coexistence, not emotionally fragmented, broken, or damaged. When we are whole, we are able for the most part to:

- Live honestly and freely as ourselves, limited only by God's love.

- Let go of our desire for power and control.

- Learn to distinguish between the voice of our ego and the voice of God's love.

- Allow others to be who they are in a compassionate, non-judgmental way.

- Allow others to disagree with us without responding with anger or shame.

- Feel focused more than fragmented.

- Be present to others.

- Resist letting our desire for security and survival have too much influence in our decision-making.

- Become more aware of when we are reacting to life rather than receiving life.

- Recognize our own limitations.

- Be grateful for difficult circumstances that move us closer to God.

- Believe that God is loving us in the present moment, whatever it holds, unconditionally.

- Notice that the fruit of the Holy Spirit is evident in our lives.

Katie, my counselor, has told me that I walk in more wholeness than anyone she knows…not that I always do life perfectly—there is no such thing—but I am attuned to God, others, and myself. What does that look like practically?

Maybe the best part is energy. My numbness and barely-present existence is in the past.

It means no major depressions for sure, not even mild ones. I can be sad over difficult losses and circumstances and leave it at that. Also, I only have a very slight reaction, or none at all, to a triggering event.

Probably the most profound benefit is genuinely releasing my loved ones and their problems into the sovereign hands of God and knowing that He is able to bring them further into Kingdom living through their pain and sufferings. Giving up on my expectations for results allows me to walk in freedom. As difficult as it can be for me to watch, I can now see how He is working all things together for their good. (Well, most of the time.) If He provided for me in the way that He did, then I know He will also provide for them.

I can also be in the present moment instead of in my obsessive thinking while someone is talking to me. This allows me to genuinely listen to their heart as well as their words. It's so wonderful not to be worried about the next word I'm going to say, missing part of what is being said because I'm trying to figure out if it is safe to speak—and if so, what to say.

My other inner world observation is being able to care for my own soul in a culture that does not value that. If you remember, I was so afraid of genuine intimacy with Christ that I would study, pray at Him, do good works—anything to still be a Christian and not intimately engage. The more healing I've received, the more still I can be. I can purposefully just "be" in His Presence, allowing for much greater intimacy in order to hear His voice and His voice alone. The fear is gone. I can sit in that sweet place of silence and just receive the love I looked for everywhere else. Actually, this is the best part of wholeness—I experience so much love and freedom in His presence.

I am able to:

- stop the negative spiraling thought life before I go into a black hole of shutting down.

- not have to be acknowledged for my deeds, especially the sacrificial ones, to remain secure.

- not promote myself into arenas where I would have authority, but wait on God to bring those opportunities to me.

- deal with the messiness of not having closure. In other words, just letting situations be what they are. They don't have to be resolved for me to have peace.

- not have to make sure everyone is calm, secure, and safe. Trusting that their issues are between them and God and release them into God's care.

- make mistakes without beating myself up or trying to make everything right again. I no longer take on too much responsibility or condemnation for something I did.

- evaluate and recognize my personal capacity for what to take on and what not to take on.

- ask for whatever kind of help I need when I need it.

- lament and grieve appropriately, i.e. equal to the event.

My "before and after" are illustrated in the chart on the next page.

Before	*After*
Irrational fear	Appropriate fear
Driven to "be" something; prove my worth	Calm and peace; accepted by God
Cannot make mistakes	Laugh about mistakes
Performance based: have to do things right "or else"	Believe who God says I am
Black & white thinking	Consider all my options
Opposing/battling thoughts	Can think things through
People-pleasing to create my own safety	Feel safe whether people are happy with me or not
Paranoia/people are against me	People probably think well of me
Disorientation/Confusion	Clear thinking
Lack of organization and organized thinking	Keep my life fairly orderly
Need to control my environment	Can relax
Extreme eating habits	Healthy eating
Extreme clean or extreme mess	Appropriate/not obsessive
Blame others	Trust they have good hearts
Extreme self-condemnation	Give myself grace
Nightmares	Dreams are current, helpful
Anger—out of proportion to events	Grace and love
Thoughts of violence or paranoia	Safe and secure
Thoughts of insanity	Able to stand in truth
Suicidal	Love myself

One of the first times I saw the fruit of pursuing healing was when my husband had an overreaction about how some money was spent and just "went off" on me. Instead of receiving the accusatory words, taking them straight into my heart and mind and believing them, I was able to walk away without saying a thing and tell myself, "Whew, that's his problem." It was clear he was overreacting, which meant it was his own issue. In that moment I knew: it works, it really works to deal with your history, and it provides genuine freedom.

Two incidents with my daughter show the sharp contrast before and after my healing.

My daughter and her then-boyfriend announced they were engaged when they were nineteen. They wanted to come over to our house for dinner. After we had finished, she stood up, walked over to stand beside him, held up her left hand and said, "We're engaged…and I'm pregnant."

I remember it taking at least five minutes for me to speak, and then all I could genuinely say was, "Thank you for not getting an abortion." Somehow, I made it through the rest of the evening without shutting down, but then went to bed for three full days. I had no other coping method. All I could do was spiral down into depression.

Then about sixteen or eighteen years later, they decided she was going to be a surrogate. For a myriad of reasons, I was very disappointed and disagreed with their decision. We were able to talk it over and agree to disagree, and I did not go into depression because of her choices. As soon as she conceived, I knew it had to be God's will. She had twins and we get to be a small part of their lives and thoroughly enjoy them.

There's a love, a peace, a joy, a belonging, and a security that I can function out of now. Because it's a journey and not a destination, I'm still in process.

The love is feeling secure in the unconditional love of God even when people cannot offer me their love.

The peace comes from the love and security that I don't have to perform anymore for anybody—not that I can't occasionally fall into it, but it's rare. I know that, even if I don't do it right, I can give myself grace and know that everything will still work out.

Having replaced so many lies with so much truth, I am able to stand in the truth of who I am, who others are, and who God is, most of the time. There is a congruence in my inner being that I rest in, rather than stewing in anxiety. It is hard to explain, but when I walk in a room of strangers, no matter who is there, I know I am an equal but can still always aim to think of others as better than myself.

Here is another example. We were all at this milestone family birthday party with lots of family and guests. I was having a one-on-one conversation with a family member off to the side. It was not intense, but it was about a difficult situation they were dealing with. All of a sudden, this person grabbed my head between his hands, while spewing accusatory remarks, unloading both barrels. Let me say, it was way out of character. Later, I realized they were under more stress than I realized. The incredible thing—it did not phase me. I did not take it personally, I knew it was their problem, and I was able to ENJOY the party.

Normally I would have been devastated, unable to enjoy the party, and gone into a coma-like state for the rest of the evening. I would have pretended to enjoy myself, but I would have beat myself up, believing the lies that I had done something wrong or could not please them. The contrast felt victorious.

One more: recently my daughter-in-law's parents moved to our town. Instead of being threatened and fearful of being excluded, like I would have been in the past, I am able to embrace them with open arms and include them. Most of all, I can be truly happy and thankful that my daughter-in-law has her parents to enjoy for the first time in their married life. For Christmas her Mom gave me a tea towel that says, "All are welcome here." And in my heart, it is true.

Of all the gifts, the greatest gift of all is being able to comfort others with the comfort I have been given.

I have sat with countless people in their pain and suffering with a compassionate ear, listening heart, and a powerful way of hearing from God that brings genuine, tangible, emotional relief and healing. To sit in that sacred place as a friend and wounded healer has been my greatest privilege (other than parenting two incredible children).

I have also been able to counsel my grandchildren as they try to navigate their teen years. I tell them the hardest job in the world is being a parent, but the second hardest is being a teenager. They know I will listen to them in a non-judgmental way.

My daughter told me that at their house, they all say, "Nobody loves like Nana." What a legacy I've been given.

Henri Nouwen says it this way:

> "To enter into solidarity with a suffering person does not mean that we have to talk with that person about our own suffering. Speaking about our own pain is seldom helpful for someone who is in pain. A wounded healer is someone who can listen to a person in pain without having to speak about his or her own wounds. When we have lived through a painful depression, we can listen with great attentiveness and love to a depressed friend without mentioning our experience. Mostly it is better not to direct a suffering person's attention to ourselves. We have to trust that our own bandaged wounds will allow us to listen to others with our whole beings. That is healing."

The frosting on the cake is living in the present moment enough to slow down and walk through the grocery store so when you politely exchange courtesies with the woman stacking shelves, she ends up sharing her broken heart. You pray, telling her God sees her, and are able to speak God's heart into her situation.

How do I feel now about my life? There is an exercise in the Transformational Prayer Healing Seminar I attended where we were led to picture ourselves with God before we were born.

I pictured being somewhere in this vast universe of stars and planets, beauty, and peace. The Lord was there with me, all at a time before I existed. He showed me what my life with my parents would be, then asked me if I wanted to go live it. He asked my permission to put the egg and the sperm together that would result in the creation of me. I said, "No way in hell." Then He began to show me the end of the story, the resurrection and redemption. I listened and was able to say, "Yes, yes, I will go."

I'm truly humbled by the lovingkindness, mercy, and grace of a God who faithfully carried me through all those years of dysfunction and brought me out on this side.

With God, all things really are possible.

To God Be The Glory

Appendices

Appendix 1: The Problem

In my time with my counselor, looking at my own story, along with my years of training and experience in Inner Healing Prayer, I discovered why people are the way they are. David Benner describes it in the following way:

> Genuinely transformational knowing of self always involves encountering and embracing previously unwelcome parts of self. While we tend to think of ourselves as a single, unified self, what we call "I" is really a family of many part-selves. That in itself is not a particular problem. The problem lies in the fact that many of these part-selves are unknown to us. Even though they are usually known to others, we remain blissfully oblivious of their existence.

> To say that we are a family of many part-selves is not the same as saying that we play different roles. Most of us know what it is to be a friend, employee, church member, and possibly a parent or a spouse. Each of these roles is different, and most of us can move between them effortlessly. This is not the problem.

The problem is that there are important aspects of our experience that we ignore…When we do so, however, these unwanted parts of self, do not go away. They simply go into hiding.

If, for example, I only know my strong, competent self and am never able to embrace my weak or insecure self, I am forced to live a lie. I must pretend that I am strong and competent, not simply that I have strong and competent parts or that under certain circumstances I can be strong and competent. Similarly, if I refuse to face my deceitful self, I live an illusion regarding my own integrity. Or if I am unwilling to acknowledge my prideful self, I live an illusion of false modesty.

(THE GIFT OF BEING YOURSELF by David Benner)

Our capacity for freedom of choice and action is limited by our bondage to personality factors that operate beyond our awareness. In other words, it is that which we choose not to know or acknowledge about ourselves i.e. that which we repress, deny or in other ways relegate to the unconscious that has the most power over us….the more such things exist and the more unwilling we are to face them, the greater the bondage.

(CARE OF SOULS by David Benner)

***

The deeper goal of Inner Healing Prayer: to help every inner-child part of the self that was necessary to survive childhood to become integrated into the adult.

As you become an adult those child-like parts will constantly be triggered and try to do life for you and that is why life does not work.

In everyday life, we live out of the frontal lobe of our brain. We are able to make decisions, accomplish tasks, relate to others, etc. The problem comes when the trauma event that remains in that closed-off unconscious part of the brain is triggered by circumstances that are similar to the original trauma experience.

The unconscious section of the brain will take priority over the logical part of the brain, the frontal lobe, and try to handle the situation it feels threatened by.

For example, an adult's inner child is stuck in a traumatic event at eight years old because their father unexpectedly passed away. They grow up, marry and have children, managing as an adult most of the time. However, trying to be a spouse, parent, make a living, and be responsible can be overwhelming. The adult tries to cope with the overwhelmed feeling by using some dysfunctional behavior—anger, depression, drugs, drinking, eating, pornography, obsessive compulsive behavior or all of the above.

It is really the inner-child part that is trying to handle all the responsibilities of adult life, because the psyche is stuck there.

Oftentimes that overwhelmed feeling gets "triggered." The tendency is to "overreact" and handle the situation like an eight-year-old instead of an adult. If the reaction does not equal the event, you can know that person's history is being tapped into and they are reacting to the current event out of a place of historical wounding.

It's happening because the adult has never processed the pain that the eight-year-old was—and still is—in.

There will be times of knowing as an adult that you want to stop the way you are thinking and acting but cannot manage to do it.

A fist illustration shows what happens in the brain when we are in that stuck place.

Think of the arm as the spinal cord, the wrist as the brain stem, and the thumb as the limbic system: emotions and memories from trauma and abuse.

Think of the fingers as the frontal lobe and reasoning ability that develops later in life.

Because a little child's emotions are exaggerated, no matter what they are, the thumb (emotions) sends the messages to the fingers. The thumb gets triggered or stirred up and the child doesn't have reasoning ability yet. If you are an adult, your reasoning ability can get frozen.

If the rational part of the brain, the prefrontal cortex adult is in control, the fingers can send the messages down to the thumb or emotions.

An example might be opening the refrigerator and seeing a snake inside. The thumb/limbic system/emotions will want to run out of the house and burn the whole house down.

Instead, the fingers—the rational part of the brain—can wrap themselves over the thumb and send adult messages to the limbic system. Then the response is, "I'll just close the refrigerator door and call someone for help."

Here is another example when the emotional part of my brain (thumb) was triggered. I was trying to rescue a teenager from a difficult situation he was in. The texting went something like this.

"I'm scared, would you come get me?"

"Where are you? What are you doing?"

"In a fight, don't want to call my parents please come!!"

"OK, text me the address."

When I arrived, he got in the car and was crying so hard he was unable to get control. I was so angry that he was in that state, I said things I shouldn't have, including criticizing the parents. They heard about it later and were angry with me.

My next Inner Healing Prayer appointment revealed that a hurting child is a trigger for me. I overreacted, went into savior mode, and tried to rescue—offending the parents in the process. Because I was rightly accused of rescuing, it meant I had failed. So I believed the lie, again, that I cannot do it right. I emotionally shut down for days.

Instead of my fingers sending messages to my thumb or emotions about the situation, my thumb was sending messages to my fingers. The thumb—the dissociated self-parts—were in control.

Going to the memory in the same session revealed a five-year-old part of me who tried to keep the peace and rescue my siblings. But of course, I was powerless to do anything. The Lord showed me I believed the following lies:

- I have to keep the peace.

- Now is the same as back then.

- I cannot connect with God and use the rational part of the brain.

- My only safe place is to shut down and go into depression.

After I connected with God during the session, He showed me the truth:

- My safe place was hiding under the shadow of His wings, not going numb.

- I could ask God to make a new pathway in my brain to the truth.

- I could choose not to view current trauma as the same as back then.

- I could bring the fingers down over the thumb.

- He equipped me to connect with Him and forgive those that have hurt me, including myself.

- It is not my job to keep the peace or make everybody happy.

When it happens again, I know I will not repeat the same mistake.

> There is enormous value in naming and coming to know these excluded parts of self... Christian spirituality involves acknowledging all our part-selves, exposing them to God's love and letting him weave them into the new person He is making. To do this, we must be willing to welcome these ignored parts as full members of the family of self, giving them space at the family table and slowly allowing them to be softened and healed by love and integrated into the whole person we are becoming.
>
> THE GIFT OF BEING YOURSELF by David Benner

The true self.

Appendix 2: Self-Care

My other discoveries in this healing journey provided new ways to practice self-care. God gifted me with a special grace and also enabled me to love and care for myself.

Wholeness takes time. I have to remember how long it took for me to get here.

> Above all, trust in the slow work of God. We are quite naturally impatient in everything to reach the end without delay. We should like to skip the intermediate stages. We are impatient of being on the way to something unknown, something new. And yet it is the law of all progress that it is made by passing through some stages of instability—and that it may take a very long time. And so I think it is with you' your ideas mature gradually—let them grow, let them shape themselves, without undue haste. Don't try to force them on, as though you could be today what time (that is to say, grace and circumstances acting on your own good will) will make of you tomorrow. Only God could say what this new spirit gradually forming within you will be. Give Our Lord the benefit of believing that his hand is leading you, and accept that anxiety of feeling yourself in suspense and incomplete.

by Pierre Teilhard de Chardin, SJ from <u>Hearts on Fire</u>

If God had let me know everything that happened to me all at once, I would have had a psychotic break and never recovered. It was His mercy and lovingkindness that allowed it to take time.

VALUE AND LOVE YOURSELF

Counseling is a gift you give yourself. First, I had to value and love myself enough to pay for a good counselor. With no idea how I was going to pay for it sometimes, the Lord always provided. Ideally, find someone that has counseling skills combined with Inner Healing Prayer. Pray and ask God to lead you to the right people. It may take a few tries, but He will.

Pastor Brent, the first one who suggested that I had some "dissociative part," suggested three counselors. I called all three and the first one to call back was Laura, the one who was beginning to understand Inner Healing Prayer.

There are some other practices that I learned along the way that were surprisingly helpful.

COMMUNITY

Surround yourself with a community whose priorities are looking to Christ with love and seeking His Presence above all else: people who strive to live full of grace, love, acceptance, and forgiveness. You need a community where you feel safe to be who you are while being heard, understood, and supported. At the same time, remember that we are all flawed human beings.

There is a fine balance between good healthy community and looking for an earthly savior. I found myself going from person to person to person for help. That is not healthy. As survivors of any kind of abuse, we tend to do that. It's time to stop and ask the Lord how and where to get professional help.

RECEIVE ATTUNEMENT FROM THE LORD

This method is from Dr. Karl Lehman's book, Outsmarting Yourself. You can also read his essays online for free. Here is a brief overview of part of his essay entitled "Brain Science, Psychological Trauma and the God Who is With Us:"

> Attunement is perceiving that someone is with us in our pain; perceiving that this person is glad to be with us; feeling that this person hears, understands, and empathizes with us in our pain. Choosing to receive this attunement will smoothly, quickly, and consistently bring our relational connection circuits back online.

Unfortunately, friends with the capacity and maturity skills necessary for being with us in our pain and offering attunement are often not conveniently available when we are most in need of this kind of help.

The Lord is always with us, and glad to be with us, especially in our pain. He always cares, and he always hears, understands, and empathizes with us.

Steps include:

- Initial prayer...thanking Him for His presence in my pain

- Recall a positive memory of a previous connection with the Lord where it felt true that you were having a living, real-time, mutual, contingent interaction with Him. It may feel faint, but try to recreate your "Safe Place" with Him.

- Re-enter this memory with Him as much as possible for a minute or two to recreate the brain-mind-spirit state as much as possible.

(Since I journal most of mine, I can even go back and reread what I wrote about it. The reason we re-enter the memory of a previous interactive connection is that this seems to provide an especially good context for establishing an interactive connection in the present.)

- Transition to living, real time, interactive connection in the present.

(Simply, ask if His presence in the memory feels like it's only a memory, or does it feel like He's with me in the present, as a living presence? The answer will always be that He is with me in the present.)

- Talk to the Lord about your pain. Thank Him for His presence.

(This includes temporarily letting go of trying to manage the pain and just letting yourself feel it. Use words for what feels true with respect to the pain in order to describe it. Then share this with the Lord as clearly, honestly, and vulnerably as possible.)

- Receive the Lord's attunement. It will always be words of comfort, encouragement, and His love toward us.

"STOP" EXERCISE

Let's say you have an overreaction and are emotionally stirred up…it's difficult to calm yourself…nothing else seems to be working. This exercise will help you to stop focusing on the issue, current event, or trigger. It sounds silly, but is actually therapeutic.

1. Feel the feeling first instead of focusing on the issue/incident. Be internally present – what am I feeling? Name it.

2. Put your hand out and up – say stop, stop, stop three times.

3. Focus on a spot on the wall.

4. Put the thumb up on your right hand.

5. Smile really big.

6. Hold both hands out and down, moving them like a river.

7. Say "I did it!" "I did it!" "I did it!"

8. Speak out loud the truth over yourself. Speak whatever God is saying to you in the moment.

If you cannot hear truth, then repeat the exercise until you begin to hear it. This is a simple exercise to retrain and reroute the circuits in your brain, help restore it to an easy, gentle normal, bringing it back into balance instead of being in that fight-or-flight mode.

SPEAKING TRUTH OVER YOURSELF/AFFIRMATIONS

Here are some more truths you can speak over yourself. Repeat as much as necessary. The truth will calm down the internal turmoil.

"That was then. This is now." This may be the most important thing to say.

The gospel is: "God loves me as I am, not as I should be."

"I am good enough as I am."

"I love and approve of myself."

"I am safe."

"I belong."

"I am doing the best I can."

"It is OK for me to express myself freely."

Practice staying focused in the present moment.

Repeat any verses that you find helpful.

Name all the people that you know who love you, one by one. "_____ loves me."

Appendix 3: Basic Inner Healing Prayer Process

The following is an overview of the Inner Healing Prayer Process:

STEP 1 – SAFE PLACE

Center yourself by taking a few deep breaths. You are here to "Be still and know that He is God" (Psalm 46:10). Rest. Breathe. Relax.

Imagine your favorite place. Maybe it's a beach, a stream, or a favorite chair. It's just for you but it represents a personal, peaceful safe place.

Ask Jesus for His thoughts toward you or what is on His heart about you right now in this moment. You need not fear, it will only be something positive. He cannot be anything but LOVE. He cannot love you any less or any more than He already does.

Any voice or thought you have that is negative is not from Him.

Then, if you want to—and only if you want to—ask Jesus to come into that place. (Some people will have reasons not to feel safe with Jesus there.)

This provides a positive way to connect with Him. Most people experience Him in a safe place by seeing Him or sensing His Presence as a feeling of warmth, peace, and light. A symbolic representation like a cross, a lamb, or a flower may come to mind.

Wait and listen. Journal whatever comes to mind even if you think it might be "wrong."

STEP 2 – A RECENT EVENT OR EMOTION

Ask Jesus to bring to mind a recent event, an emotion you've struggled with, a dysfunctional behavior, or something he was highlighting in the safe place.

It may be a recurring painful emotion, a general sadness or depression, a constant fear you deal with, guilt that keeps surfacing, shame or addiction, an area of bondage.

(Pay special attention to an emotion involving a recent event where you may have overreacted or underreacted to an event. If your response is not equal to the event, you can know it is coming out of your history. You've just been triggered.)

Welcoming the emotion is the first step toward inner healing. Once you acknowledge it and let it be what it is, it will release what your mind and body are feeling.

A couple ways you can begin to do that:

1. Bring all of your attention to the physical sensation of your emotion. Allow it. Sink into it. Do not try to change it. Welcome it. No analyzing. Avoid heading into the narrative of your justification. Our thought patterns are so ingrained, we automatically go to the argument instead of acknowledging the emotion.

2. Name the emotion or physical sensation as best you can. You don't welcome the abuse, the cancer, the death of a loved one or the person putting you down in front of everybody—you just welcome whatever emotion comes up.

3. I often use "The Welcome Prayer" by Thomas Keating:

Welcome, Welcome, Welcome.

I welcome everything that comes to me in this moment because I know it is for my healing.

I welcome all thoughts, feelings, emotions, persons, situations, and conditions.

I let go of my desire for power and control,

My desire for security and survival,

My desire for approval, esteem, affection and pleasure.

I let go of my desire to change any situation, condition, person or myself.

I open to the love and presence of God and His healing action

And grace within.

Sometimes I just repeat the first two sentences over and over until I feel more in touch with the emotion and more centered. Do not be afraid of it. We believe it will overwhelm us and we won't be able to handle it if we let it come, but that is a lie.

Connecting with emotions is like a depression vaccine.

After naming the emotion, acknowledging it for what it is, Inner Healing Prayer will offer the greatest relief.

Take as much time as you need. You never need to feel rushed. This process is slow moving.

STEP 3 – THE MEMORY

Ask the Lord for a memory, showing you where you first felt that same emotion. We ask for the earliest one because it is the root place. Ideally, if you move through the Inner Healing Prayer process in the memory of the event, you will be set free from the beliefs and behavior patterns.

Pray for only as much as you need to know, no more and no less. When He brings the memory to your awareness, remember you are present here and now. Say to yourself "That was then and this is now." You don't have to go back to then, just observe the scene. He will never give us more than we can handle.

Ask Him where He was and how He was feeling when that was happening to you. He will show you.

STEP 4 – BELIEFS

The memory is important, but not as important as what you came to believe about yourself, God, or others in that event. Ask God to reveal what you came to believe in that memory, and He will tell you exactly. Journal all that He reveals to you. What you came to believe can be one or several of the following:

LIE – Children are wonderful observers but terrible interpreters. So, we come up with these "I am…" statements from influential events in our lives. An adult can observe the same situation and know it is not harmful, but a child can take it into their heart and mind and misinterpret it. For example, a child who spends a lot of time alone can begin to believe that "I am not worth loving. I am unlovable." A bad experience in the classroom, and someone can come away believing "I am stupid."

VOW – As a child, you may have made yourself a solemn promise for future self-protection: "I will never be vulnerable again," or, "I will never be like my mother."

PRONOUNCEMENT – A curse. This is a statement someone speaks over you, or that you speak over yourself, that has come to define who you are. "You are so lazy." "You are worthless." "You will never amount to anything."

PATTERN – A recurring theme you grew up with: "Children are to be seen and not heard." Perfectionism is huge for a lot of people. Maybe everything you said was discounted, leading to a pattern of believing "I do not have a voice."

BURDEN – Something you are carrying that is not yours to carry. You may have felt responsible for a parent or for siblings growing up.

STRATEGY – A way you decided to do life because of the memories and beliefs…like being a perfectionist, or not letting people get too close emotionally.

Take plenty of time to journal anything the Lord reveals.

STEP 5 – A PRAYER TO BREAK THE BELIEF

Break or renounce the beliefs by saying the following prayer out loud:

In the name, power and authority of the true Lord Jesus Christ of Nazareth,

I break the lie that_____

I break the vow that_____

I break the pronouncement that_____

I break the pattern of _____

I hand over the burden of _____

I break the strategy that _____

and I break how that has affected my life emotionally, physically, spiritually, financially, sexually, in all my relationships, in my world view, life, blood and death, power and control, ownership and leadership and in every other way. I break it all the way down to the RNA, DNA, cellular and molecular levels.

I command any spirits including the original demonic spirit, "Leave and go where the true Lord Jesus Christ of Nazareth tells you to go. You cannot stay, and you cannot return to any of our family, friends, or ministries."

STEP 6 – TRUTH

Ask God to replace the lies, vows, pronouncements, patterns, burdens, or strategies with His truth. When He does that, it is immediate, miraculous healing, because it is in the very place where the wounding occurred.

It's like having a foundation of building blocks. Each one is a lie, so you begin to take them out one at a time and replace each one with a block of truth. Instead of a foundation of lies, you can begin to live on a foundation of truth.

"The thief comes only to kill, steal and destroy. I came that they may have life and have it abundantly." John 10:10

***

There is a deeper level of Inner Healing Prayer that is used when it becomes necessary for a dissociated part of the self to receive healing. Some of the most profound healing I received involved Reparenting.

REPARENTING

Reparenting is the process of the adult self-ministering to the inner child or the "little you" on the inside that experienced the abuse. The adult self-parents the inner child, providing the healthy parenting that they never received.

My counselor would walk me through the Inner Healing Prayer process and then add this dimension of reparenting. It is possible to do this process on your own while journaling your responses, but I recommend having someone guide you through it. This is a general example. Jesus knows we are uniquely created and He ministers to us exactly the way we need to be ministered to.

1. Identify the emotion or trigger that is causing the internal struggle. Name it: fear, pain, loss, hurt, anger.

2. Ask the Lord for the root memory where the same emotion occurred and ask for the inner-child part that experienced the trauma. Try to get some sense of the age.

3. Use the normal Inner Healing Prayer steps, asking for the beliefs and breaking any lies, vows, etc.

a. Safe place with the Lord.

b. Identify the emotion He highlights.

c. Ask Jesus to bring a memory to mind.

d. Ask Him to show you what you came to believe in the memory.

e. Break the lies, vows, etc.

f. Ask Him to replace what you came to believe with the truth.

4. Invite Jesus into the memory. Usually, the inner child part will need something from the adult such as love, comfort, a promise of care or safety. This is where the reparenting can take place. Then, as Jesus is in the picture with the adult self and the inner child, the adult reparents the inner child:

a. Validate their feelings, support them, offer acceptance and encouragement in much the same way as a strong, nurturing parent would do for their child.

b. It's possible for the inner child to be mad or upset with the adult. Sometimes a reconciliation needs to take place. Jesus is there to help them work through their pain in a patient and gentle way.

c. The adult might need to ask for forgiveness for whatever the inner child is offended about—such as not caring for them, not protecting them, not wanting them, i.e. "I hate that part of myself."

5. Ask the inner child if there is anything else they need. It might be a symbol of something comforting—a blanket, a doll, a promise. Follow what the Lord is revealing.

6. Ask the inner child if they would like to know the comfort of Jesus. He will show them that they can rest or play if they are willing to go and be with Him. I often had a vision of being in a field of flowers where Jesus would be kneeling with His arms open, waiting for me to come. The inner child is usually ready to go and be with Jesus.

7. When the inner child chooses to go and be with Jesus, it is integration! That is the goal. I experienced several sessions with the reparenting component, and they ended up being the most powerful healing moments of my life.